The comunity at prayer, monastery of Saint Stephen,
Ravenna - Italy.
Photo by Riccardo Palazzi

CLOISTERED CARMEL

A BRIEF HISTORY OF THE CARMELITE NUNS

by

JOACHIM SMET, O.CARM.

INSTITUTUM CARMELITANUM

Roma 1986

The passages by Stefan Hilpisch, O.S.B., quoted
in chapter I, are taken from his *History of Benedictine Nuns*, copyright © 1958 by The Order of
St. Benedict, Inc. Published by The Liturgical Press,
Collegeville, Minnesota. Used with permission.

The material for this book is taken almost entirely from the author's general history, *The Carmelites*, Darien, Ill., Carmelite Spiritual Center, 1975-
1985, 4 v. in 5, to which the reader interested in the
sources is referred.

ISTITUTUM CARMELITANUM

Via Sforza Pallavicini, 10
00193 Roma

To

LORETTA, HELEN, VIRGINIA, FRANCES, JULIANNA

who all wanted to be nuns

Tip. De Magistris & Ceccacci - Via G. di Tuscolo, 40-42
00046 Grottaferrata (Roma) - Tel. 945.84.69

CONTENTS

CONTENTS

Chapter I

THE CARMELITE SISTERS
IN THE MIDDLE AGES

Whatever is to be said about woman's role in the ministries of the Church, the part she has played in that particular expression of Christian faith known as the religious life is in every way equal to that of men. The following of Christ was not confined to apostles and disciples, nor did Jesus limit his attentions to men. The faith and devotion of women among the associates of the Master have been touchingly recorded in the writings of the New Testament.

While we must wait until the fourth century for the rise of monasticism among men, the institution of "consecrated virgins" recommended by Saint Paul (*1 Cor. 7, 8*), is as old as Christianity itself. From Tertullian we learn that these virgins recited the psalms. In the third century, like married women, they took to wearing a veil, conferred on them by the bishop, who also received their vow of virginity. The virgin consecrated to Christ was held in honor in the community, she had a special place in church, her state of life was recognized in the bidding prayers. Her particular function in the community, apart from the witness of her life, became the care of the poor and the instruction and baptism of women catechumens. These tasks and the fact that she owed allegiance to the bishop constituted her as the female counterpart to the clergy, whose way of life moreover resembled hers in externals. The liberation of Christianity by Constantine (*d.* 337) made possible religious life in community. Alongside monasteries of men rose those of women which attracted many women desirous of the consecrated celibate life. The virgins underwent a decline and disappeared by the ninth century, to be replaced by the institution of canon-esses.

Saint Pachomius of Tabennisi (*d.* 346) is credited with founding the first monastery in modern form, for which he also wrote a rule. Nearby he founded another monastery for women under his sister Mary (*ca.* 330). The rule of Pachomius enjoyed great success, and nunneries arose in Egypt, Syria, Palestine, and Asia Minor. Of this sort were the three monasteries founded in Bethlehem by the noble Roman matron Paula (*d.* 404) and her daughter Eustochium, spiritual daughters of St. Jerome. St. Basil (*d.* 379) also founded a monastery and gave it a rule adapted from his rule for monks.

In the West, where monasteries for women began to appear at the end of the fourth century, the rule of St. Augustine held sway. Cassian, famed author of *Conferences* for monks (*d. ca.* 435), was the spiritual director of a nunnery in Marseille. Gaul, where Christianity had early taken root, soon became populated with nunneries. Caesarius of Arles (*d.* 542) wrote a rule for the monastery of Arles of which his sister Caesaria was superior. An important innovation introduced by Caesarius was the *clausura* or enclosure. This rule was widely accepted in the Gallic monasteries, prominent among which was that of Poitiers, where Queen Radigund lived, and of which the poet Venantius Fortunatus was spiritual director from 542 to 562. It was on the occasion of the transfer of a relic of the Holy Cross to this monastery that he wrote his well-known hymn *Vexilla regis prodeunt*. The appearance in Gaul of St. Columban (*d.* 615) introduced the influence of Irish monasticism. Of this trend was the rule written by Donatus, bishop of Besançon (*d.* 656), for the monastery governed by his mother Flavia. Already in the fourth century Spain knew religious life for women; it appeared in Ireland a century later. At the end of the fourth century the Spanish nun Aetheria wrote her noted account of her pilgrimage to the Holy Land, a valuable witness to the liturgical usages of the early Church.

Religious life was an important factor in fostering the new dignity which Christianity conferred on women. "To remain unmarried," writes Dom Stefan Hilpisch, "was no longer a misfortune, much less a disgrace; on the contrary, virginity ranked high in meaning and purpose. Here was a new evaluation of the personality of woman. She did not require a husband to be esteemed and through him to find the fulness of life within the family. Indeed, the virgin could even attain a higher dignity than the married woman. As the latter received her dignity through the wealth and position of her husband, so the virgin received hers through religious consecration and through Christ the Lord, to whom she was espoused.

"In the ascetic life woman received the opportunity for suitable self-development and a corresponding mission, work in a convent, with a community of sisters banded together for the same lofty purpose. Within this community, thanks to her womanhood, she could work out the virtues of humility, love and chastity much more readily and purely than it is given men to do."

The nun of early monasticism was frequently a noblewoman, even royalty, and was an educated woman, by no means intellectually inferior to the monk. "How could the intellectual life have been neglected," Dom Hilpisch continues, "when Ambrose, Jerome, Augustine and Rufinus were the spiritual fathers of the nuns! It was the women who listened to them most eagerly. Many ascetical and theological problems which challenged the teachers of the fourth century were first discussed with the nuns. Jerome made it clear that the true nun is a student; his letter on the education of Laeta was the foundation for the later development of the intellectual life in convents."

From what has been said so far it will be clear that religious life for women in its early period was in no way uniform. There were many rules and many ways of observing them. All this changed after the sixth century, when St. Benedict, "the Father of Western Monasticism," wrote his classic rule, which became the norm for nuns as well as monks. In the thirteenth century the Mendicant Orders introduced a new form of religious life based on the ideal of poverty.

9

Among the many unsolved mysteries of Carmelite history is the question, why it took Carmel so long to accept cloistered life for women. While the other Mendicant Orders, Franciscans, Dominicans, Augustinians, Servites, almost immediately initiated this institution, the Carmelites waited until the fifteenth century to do so. Perhaps the little known rule of St. Albert lacked the attraction of the famous Benedictine, Augustinian, and Franciscan rules. In Italy at least an explanation may be found in the flourishing state of other forms of affiliating women to the Order.

The history of Carmelite nunneries resembles that of feminine monasticism in general, in that it was preceded by a lengthy period during which women also followed the rule of Carmel outside community, somewhat as had the consecrated virgins before the rise of monasticism.

In order to follow the gamut of Carmelite life in the Middle Ages one must divest one's mind of the modern forms in which that life finds expression. To use terms until recently current, Carmelites today are grouped into five clearly defined categories: First Order (friars), Second Order (nuns with solemn vows), Third Order Regular (sisters with simple vows), Third Order Secular (lay persons who follow a rule adapted to their state in life), Confraternity of Our Lady of Mount Carmel (wearers of the brown scapular). The numerical designation of the branches of the Order (First, Second, Third) originated with the Order of Humiliates and was not applicable to the Carmelites, who only later adopted it. One will search in vain for a Carmelite Third Order in the Middle Ages, though its equivalent existed.

Apart from the friars (professed members, living in community) Carmelite life in the Middle Ages, reflecting contemporary religious practice generally, was a coat of many hues. The friars constituted the fraternity (*fraternitas*); the essential element of their habit was the scapular. All other members, whatever the degree of their affiliation, expressed by different names, formed the confraternity (*confraternitas*), not to be confused with the modern technical use of the word. Confraternity simply meant: added to the fraternity (in various ways). The typical habit of this class of Carmel was the white mantle (*signum professionis*, sign of profession), hence in Italy the name "mantellates." Only in the fifteenth century did lay Carmelites begin, at first under their clothing, to wear the scapular. Such a practice would have made no sense to the medieval mind. The degree of affiliation to the Order depended on the obligations assumed. The most attenuated form of affiliation was that of benefactors who in return for their largesse received "letters of affiliation," which entitled them to a share in the spiritual benefits of the Order.

Affiliation of women developed most extensively in Italy.

We may distinguish first of all the *conversae*, or oblates. They were the forerunners of the cloistered nuns and to all intents and purposes differed from the friars only in that they did not live in the convent. They were in fact subject to the prior, to whom they made their oblation, and were members of his community.

A very early instance of oblation occurs in Messina in 1283, when Bonaventura di Misano solemnly vowed chastity to the Carmelite community, bestowing on it all her goods and receiving in return a portion of their usufruct for her modest needs. At Bologna in 1304 Benvenuta Venturoli pledged herself and her goods (*se et sua*) to the prior of the Carmelite convent of St. Martin, promising him obedience, as became a *conversa* or oblate. The prior assigned her her former house as her place of residence, for religious vows presupposed *stabilitas*, or attachment to a fixed habitation. In 1309, Diana Buzzadelli, desirous of spending the rest of her life in obedience to holy religion, offered herself and her possessions to the prior of the Carmine of Florence, vowing him obedience according to the rule and constitutions of Carmel, as required of a "true *conversa* and subject." Other examples of oblation or conversion are those of Santa Saluccio, also of Florence, in 1374, and of Bonuccia Sardi, of Pisa, in 1390.

11

An interesting case is that of Salvino degli Armati and of his wife Bartolomea, of Florence, who simultaneously entered the Order as oblates. In May, 1343, they pronounced the three vows to God, Our Lady of Mount Carmel, and the superiors of the Carmelite Order according to its rule and constitutions until death. The provincial of Tuscany conferred on them the habit of the Order and enrolled Salvino among the *conversi*, or laybrothers, who in fact were the male equivalent of the *conversae*. Bartolomea, of course, because of her sex could not live in the convent.

The oblation of the *conversae* fulfilled all the requirements of contemporary canon law for religious vows. According to a legal saw then current, any of four conditions sufficed for religious vows: sacred orders, a document, spontaneous profession, or reception of the habit of the professed. Nicolò de Tudeschi, authoritative seventeenth century glossator, called the "Panormitan," declares that when "women professing the rule of men" make their vows in their hands, they are to be considered "true religious," even though they do not enter a monastery of nuns but remain in what was once their own home. Such vows were solemn vows, the only sort of religious vow known at the time. Although Boniface VIII in 1298 imposed cloister on the monasteries, this prescription was for the most part more honored in the breach than in the observance. Not until the Council of Trent (1545-1563) did cloister become a requirement for solemn vows.

In the thirteenth and fourteenth centuries there are vague references even to communities of Carmelite nuns (*moniales*), but their status and relation to the Order are not clear.

Another class of women associated with Carmel was that of sisters, or *sorelle*, variously called *vestite, mantellate, pinzocchere* — the last name being also used to designate *converse*. These women took all or some of the three vows of poverty, chastity, and obedience, but not according to the rule of the Order (*certa regula*), hence their vows were private or simple. Unlike the *conversae* they ten-

12

ded to organize and form associations. In Venice such a group was accepted into the Order by the prior general, Gerard of Bologna, in 1300, though the "ladies and sisters" in question may have been *conversae*. Several rules followed by associations of non-professed sisters have come down: Brescia (1453), Bologna, Mantua (*ca.* 1460, composed by Bl. Bartholomew Fanti), and a rule entitled *Regola de le sorelle del Ordine*, which has survived in a late Venetian copy dated 1482 and may be the model for the other rules.

The distinction between the two kinds of Carmelite sisters is demonstrated by the case of Lorenza Lambertuccio, of Florence, who in 1378 requested to pass from "the vestites of the *pinzocchere* of the Carmelite Order» to the oblates and *conversae*. The transfer took place in another ceremony, in which Lorenza offered herself and hers to God, the Blessed Virgin, and the Carmel of Florence, and promised "stability of morals and conduct, religious obedience, and due and customary obedience and chastity." The account of Lorenza's oblation reproduces the formula of profession and minutely describes the ceremony.

The fifteenth and sixteenth centuries witnessed the change from these ways of receiving women into the Order to the forms known today. In spite of the rise of the monasteries many professed sisters, or *conversae*, continued their traditional way of life. Beside the friars and nuns they came to be known, improperly, as tertiaries. In 1583 the Holy See withheld recognition of the solemnity of their vows, which were either reduced to two (chastity and obedience) or were made according to special statutes, such as the *Regolamento o statuti* (Bologna, 1591).

On the other hand the non-professed vestites or mantellates were reorganized by Sixtus IV in his bull *Mare magnum* of 1476 along the lines of the other Mendicant Third Orders. Some of these non-professed sisters, under the influence of the Sabatine Bull and the spread of the story of the scapular vision, abandoned their distinctive white mantle in favor of the scapular. These towards the end of the sixteenth century underwent enormous growth and ended by supplanting the mantellates. In 1606 Pope Paul V reserved the privileges of confraternity to the confraternity of the scapular, which became the only recognized confraternity of the Order. A final development came about when the prior general, Theodore Straccio in 1637 enrolled in the Third Order the brothers and sisters who made the vow of obedience and chastity according to their state of life; all others he consigned to the scapular confraternity (1640).

The spirituality of the oblates and *conversae* was that of the Carmelite rule which they professed. Their "conversion," their oblation of "themselves and theirs" was an option to strive after perfection. To the three vows of religion they often added a promise of "stability" in the monastic tradition. Their celibacy was absolute, and only virgins and widows were admitted into their ranks. The rules of the sisters without religious vows prescribed daily Mass, more frequent Communion, monthly meetings, lengthy prayers. Their penitential spirit was expressed by fasting, abstinence, disciplines, mortifications. They observed chastity according to their state in life.

All the sisters, of whatever kind, did not fail to reproduce in their lives that essential element of Carmelite spirituality, Marian devotion. To Mary, after God, they paid their vows, her purity was symbolized by their white mantles and imitated in their lives, often her Little Office was their prayer.

The names of the first Carmelite sisters to sanctify their lives through the rule of St. Albert are written in the Book of Life; their stories are lost in the mists of time. One of them, however, is remembered, Bl. Joan of Toulouse, an anchoress attached to the Carmelite church in Toulouse, who seems to have lived in the late fourteenth, early fifteenth century. Most likely she was a *conversa*. The young English friar, John Bale, who came to study at Toulouse in 1527, left this account:

"Saint Joan the Virgin, according to some (and this seems the more likely account), was born in the kingdom of Navarre. She was of noble lineage,

14

nobler still by her virtue, and refused the hand of a count in marriage. In honor of Our Lady she dedicated herself completely to God as an anchoress attached to the Carmelite convent of Toulouse. She led a life of dauntless penance; she spent sleepless nights in prayer. She continually taught the young members of the Order and always prayed for them, with the result that they made wonderful progress. She ate little or nothing, slept on the ground or on a bed of twigs, and eschewed the use of bed or couch. She read the whole psalter daily. She performed many miracles during her lifetime, but after her death distinguished herself by almost innumerable signs and wonders. A large book was published about her life and miracles, but someone removed it from the convent. After her death no trace of uncleanliness was found in her cell."

Blessed Joan was beatified by Pope Leo XIII in 1895.

The story of the Carmelite sisters so far has been exclusively concerned with Italy, but the existence of Bl. Joan of Toulouse already tells us that they were not confined to that country. The Carmelite convent of Toulouse in fact was the center of a confraternity of Our Lady of Mount Carmel numbering about five thousand men and women. In that region which had experienced much difficulty with heretical lay movements, such a large association in 1267 caused concern to the brother of St. Louis IX, Alphonse, Count of Toulouse, himself a benefactor of the Order and recipient of its letters of affiliation. St. Louis is also mentioned among the affiliates of the Order. He was a generous benefactor of religious and sometime after he returned from the crusades in 1254 settled the Carmelites in Paris.

Occasionally the foundation deeds of convents reveal the existence of various types of confraternity. Thus, at the foundation of the convent of Avignon (1267), the condition was made that the rights of burial of lay persons be limited to *conversi* actually living within the conventual confines. The foundation act of Aurillac (1358) provides for those who might donate themselves and theirs (*se et sua*) — in other words, oblates.

Spain in the present state of knowledge offers more examples of affiliation of men than women. On March 13, 1315, the prior general, Gerard of Bologna, granted letters of confraternity to Ferdinand Velásquez, archdeacon of Avila (*d.* 1379). This devout priest donated all his goods to the Order and for over sixty-five years lived in the convent of San Pablo de la Moraleja. A late example of oblation is Beatrix of Castile, who in 1481 turned over all her possessions to the Carmelite friary of Los Valles, receiving in return the habit of the Order from the hands of the provincial of Castile, Andrew of Avila.

The most illustrious example of confraternity is Bl. Nuno Alvarez Pereira (1360-1431), national hero of Portugal, who after a glorious military career entered the Carmo of Lisbon as a *semi-frater*. He was born at Bomjardin, the son of Don Alvaro Gonsalvez Pereira and Irena Gonsalvez do Carvalhal. At thirteen he became a page of Queen Leonora in the court of King Ferdinand I. He married Dona Eleonora d'Alvin (*d.* 1388), and from their daughter Beatrix sprang the royal line of Braganza. At the death of the king, John of Aviz led a revolt against Queen Leonora and the Castilians. Nuno led the Portuguese to victories at Aljubarrota and Valverde (1385) and become the national hero of Portuguese independence. To military prowess Nuno added a childlike faith in the Virgin Mary. In her honor, in 1389 he began the construction of a great church in Lisbon and placed it in charge of the Carmelites because of their devotion to Mary.

In 1397 the new community under Frei Gomes de Santa Maria arrived from Moura, the only other house of the Order in Portugal at the time. Nuno himself picked Frei Gomes as well as the other friars, making sure they were "good men and Portuguese, loyal to the fatherland." The statutes of the new convent, distinguished for regular observance, prescribe meditation in common twice a day (the first instance of this practice in the Order), the rite of the Holy Sepulchre, and special practices of devotion to Our Lady.

EX DISCIPULIS TH·DE VIGILIA
PINCTUS ANNO MCCCCLXXXXI

A clothing of Sisters, 15th century.
Painting by Tommaso de Vigilia, 1492.

Blessed Joan of Toulouse, "tertiary",
an early representation.
15th century fresco, Saint Felice del Benaco - Italy.

The *semi-fratres* occupied the lowest rank in conventual life and performed the menial tasks of the house. An old painting (1526) shows Bl. Nuno clothed in the tabard, the distinctive habit of the *semifrater*.

The immemorial cult of Bl. Nuno was approved by Pope Benedict XV in 1918, until Titus Brandsma (1985) the last Carmelite to be beatified.

A descendent of St. Louis, King of France, Alphonse de la Cerda (*d*. 1366) and his wife Mafalda, known to posterity as "patrons of our Order in these realms of Castile, Portugal, and Andalusia," were no doubt affiliates of some kind.

In England persons of high standing said to be affiliated with the Order include such benefactors as St. Edward I and Henry, First Duke of Lancaster. The provincial, Thomas Brome (*d*. 1380), provided the houses of the province with pictures of St. Edward. Another provincial, the famous Thomas Netter, of Walden (*d*. 1430), interested himself in joining women to the Order. Mention is made in the sources of Emma, daughter of the knight, Miles Staplyton, who lived as a recluse attached to the Carmelite convent of Norwich until her edifying death in 1422. Recluses joined to the Northampton friary were the noblewoman Alice Wabekeyn (*d*. 1426) and Margaret Hawton, the anniversary of whose death was remembered on November 17. The devout matron Agnes was a recluse in Ipswich; Alice Grawnsett, in Cambridge. All these women Netter provided with Carmelite spiritual directors, among them John Thorpe (*d*. 1440), director of Emma Stapylton. Referred to as "nuns," these Carmelite recluses may indeed have been *conversae* or oblates. There is no reason to believe that Netter was either the first or last English provincial to promote the participation of women in the life of Carmel.

The act of oblation of Salvino and Bartolomea degli Armati, of Florence, was anticipated by at least fifty years by Bruno of Bunregassen and his wife, Jutta, founders toward the end of the thirteenth century of the Carmelite friary of Cologne.

In the Low Countries Godfrey Espavanto, subprior of Valenciennes, in 1308 admitted Agnes Tue-pana (*d.* 1319) to a group of *pinzoccherae*, of which her sister Elizabeth was already a member. Catherine of Borsbeke (*d.* 1406) lived as a Carmelite recluse near Louvain.

We are near the date and place of the foundation of the first cloistered Carmels, but we have seen that this development was preceded by a long experience by women of the Carmelite way of life.

Chapter II

BLESSED JOHN SORETH
(ca 1395-1471)

In the late Middle Ages and the Renaissance the fervor of religious Orders, reflecting the general condition of Christian life in Europe, underwent a serious decline. The causes of this were many and complex.

During the sojourn of the papacy at Avignon (1309-1377) the system of ecclesiastical taxation was devised and perfected, a sign of the growing venality of the Roman Curia. In fact, the corruption of the papacy lay at the heart of the religious malaise of the times. Immediately following, and possibly a more serious evil, was the Western Schism (1378-1447), which split the allegiance of Christians between two and even three popes, disoriented men's consciences, and discredited the teaching authority of the Church. The schism sliced down through religious Orders, which followed national allegiances to pope and anti-pope, each of whom vied with the other in granting dispensations from regular observance to their faithful followers. Between 1381 and 1411 the Carmelites were split between two priors general.

The Hundred Years' War (1337-1453), fought on French soil, laid waste a large and important part of Christendom and resulted in the destruction of many churches and religious houses and in the disruption of religious observance. Monasteries and convents within city walls were protected, but those in small towns and in the open country (the majority) offered defenseless prey to marauding armies and bands of robbers.

Pestilence, a constant presence in European society until relatively recently, at this time reached epochal proportions in the Black Death of 1348, estimated by some to have destroyed half the population of Europe. Contagion spread fast in religious communities, as does now the common cold. The Carmelite convent in Avignon lost sixty-six friars; during the years 1348-1349 the Tuscan province lost one hundred. To fill the gaps in the ranks candidates were not very carefully screened. Requirements for doctoral studies were attenuated, the number of courses lowered, degrees were granted by papal indult to supply the want of teachers. Before the origin of the Tridentine seminary ignorance among the clergy was endemic. Religious were not much better; only those destined to teach in houses of study received adequate training. As a consequence they also carried the burden of much of the pastoral work. Unfortunately the idle and ignorant friar and monk, though a favorite theme, are not entirely figments of the anti-clerical imagination. Little wonder that popular religion tended to superstition and preoccupation with the externals of the faith. The Renaissance discovered pagan Greek and Roman culture and started Europe down the path of secularism.

In this climate occurred the second mitigation of the Carmelite rule in 1432. The absolute abstinence of the rule was relaxed, and the prescription of remaining in the cell or near it was explained by Pope Eugene IV to include the conventual precincts. The latter part of the mitigation, a stumbling block to reformers of the Order for centuries, was rather a declaration or explanation of the rule than a mitigation and did not affect the essence of the Carmelite way of life. Nevertheless the mitigation coming at this time was hardly a sign of the vitality of the Order. "There was indeed evident need for a dispensation," Blessed John Soreth wryly remarked about the dispensation from abstinence, "because a general illness prevailed, if not of body, then of mind; the charity of many had grown cold."

The very distress of the Church inspired in many a desire for reform "in head and members." This spirit in turn was reflected in the religious Orders, many of which undertook programs of renewal. The Carmelites, happily, are to be found among them.

The French Carmelite, Thomas Connecte (*d.* 1433), remembered in Addison's *Spectator* (n. 98), made considerable impression on contemporaries as an itinerant preacher against the evils of the times. In 1425 he founded a reformed convent at Geronde in Switzerland, but it was not until he descended into Italy with his followers that he happened upon a situation promising wider prospects of reform.

Early in the fifteenth century the spirit of renewal made itself felt in the Tuscan province, when Jacobo di Alberto (*d.* 1426) brought about the reform of the convent of Le Selve. The followers of Connecte, whose fiery denunciations of the Roman Curia had meanwhile earned him death at the stake as a heretic, settled in the convent of Mantua, which joined Le Selve and Geronde in the common cause of renewal. At first the Italian houses at least remained a part of the Tuscan province, and its members moved about indiscriminately between reformed und unreformed houses, but in 1442 Pope Eugene IV withdrew the reformed houses from the jurisdiction of the provincial, placing them immediately under the prior general. He in turn exercised his powers through a vicar, who for all practical purposes was autonomous. Thus was constituted the historic Mantuan Congregation.

One of its early members, the famous Latin poet, Bl. Baptist of Mantua (1447-1516), thus describes the ideal of the reform: "The Mantuan Congregation, rising at the inspiration of God from the sordid neglect into which practically the whole Order had fallen, strives to pattern its life and customs after the ancient Fathers." In other words, a return to the sources. Silence and the cloister were stressed. The brethren were not permitted to wander about outside the convent, and lay persons were forbidden entrance. Money was not kept privately but placed in a community chest and disbursed from there. The mitigation of the abstinence was not accepted. The Mantuan friars wore a habit of rough undyed wool, whereas the habit of the

Order in the course of the fourteenth century had come to be made of cloth dyed black. On the backs of the more worldly brethren it often assumed an expensive quality with trimmings that would have been the envy of an abbess.

Early fruits of the reform, besides Bl. Baptist of Mantua, include Bl. Angelus Mazzinghi (*d.* 1438), variously prior in Le Selve and Florence. He was a famous preacher and much sought after spiritual director. Bl. Bartholomew Fanti (*d.* 1495) spent his life in the convent of Mantua, where he directed a confraternity of mantellates, such as we considered above, and also wrote a rule for them. He was especially devoted to the Eucharist and to Our Lady.

In its independent state the Mantuan Congregation was to prove an impediment to the reform of the Order as such. By absorbing some of the best convents in northern Italy it weakened the provinces without improving their observance.

Providentially Carmel at this time was given a prior general to undertake its renewal.

John Soreth was born near Caen in Normandy and entered the Order there. At the time Normandy was under English rule and remained so until 1450. He received the doctorate at the University of Paris in 1438. His *Lectures on the Letters of St. Paul*, which he gave as a *biblicus*, are still extant in the Bibliothèque Nationale in Paris. John is supposed to have engaged in disputation and defeated the famed Doctor Ferdinand of Corduba, regarded by his contemporaries as a magician and anti-Christ. From 1440 until his election as prior general in 1451 Bl. John headed the province of Francia.

The reform of the Order became the single preoccupation of Soreth's generalate. To this purpose he was incessantly on the road, ranging across Europe from Poland to Sicily. He was so tanned by the sun that wags among the brethren called him "the Ethiopian." He walked or rode a donkey or mule, accompanied, not by a large retinue, but only by a single companion. John van Riet was his companion during a visitation of Sicily, when some of their fellow travellers were captured by Turkish pirates. Van Riet was terrified and began to lag behind. "What are you afraid of?" the general asked. "When we are captured, your talents will recommend you to the king, while I will be led away a slave." This glimpse of Bl. John's sense of humor provides an insight into his character not otherwise afforded by his stern duties as a reformer.

Due to a lack of sources and adequate study the extent of Soreth's reform cannot at present be determined. Although he scored his greatest success in the Lower German province, it is probably safe to say that he managed to reform some convents in most provinces. Under a vicar appointed by the prior general these reformed convents remained united to their respective provinces. In Italy Soreth favored the Mantuan Congregation, of which he was gratefully acknowledged "the promotor, father, and enthusiastic supporter," but he did not confine his efforts to this group. An early product of the reform in the province of Sicily was Bl. Aloysius Rabatà (1443-1490), prior of Randazzo and martyr of charity, who never revealed the identity of his assassin.

The general chapter of Paris, 1456, promulgated Soreth's "Decree for reformed convents or those yet to be reformed in the entire Order," which Pope Callixtus III confirmed the following year. For this reason it was called "Callixtine" to distinguish it from the Mantuan Reform, called "Eugenian," because it had been established by Eugene IV.

Members of the reform, or observance, renounced all temporal goods and all privileges and exemptions. All ate at a common table. As a rule Masses outside the convent were not accepted. Visitors to the convent were admitted only with the permission of the prior. Candidates for the reform underwent a term of postulancy in secular dress at the discretion of the prior. Novices were not received before the age of eighteen; for the priesthood the age of twenty-five was required. Reformed convents had the right to elect their own prior, nor could the provincial add or remove friars from such convents without the consent of prior and community. Priors of reformed houses could receive any conventual who wished to join the reform and had wide powers of absolution from reserved sins and censures. The introduction of reform into a convent was solemnized by a special ceremony.

Blessed John did not confine his efforts at reform to promoting his observance. Among the conventuals he sought to bring about fidelity to the form of life they were actually obliged to follow. Not the least of Soreth's services to the improvement of religious life was to present the Order with an orderly, updated code of laws which remained in use until the Counter-Reformation. The constitutions of the Order had not been revised since 1369. These were a hodgepodge of capitular decrees accumulated over the years. Soreth's constitutions were promulgated at the general chapter of Brussels, 1462, approved at that of Aurillac, 1469, and first printed at Venice in 1499.

Basically the legislation of the Order remains the same, though Soreth tries to palliate some of its worst features in respect of poverty. Individual friars are granted the usufruct of immobile goods; the goods themselves belong to the community. Permission of the prior is required to retain mobile goods of even the slightest value. These may no longer be disposed of by testament at death. Exception is made for officials like prior general, provincials and procurators, who may leave books and other mobile goods to communities or students. Expressions denoting ownership, like " buying" or "selling" are avoided. Cells may be "procured" by individuals or assigned to their use. No distinction is any longer made between needy and well-to-do friars.

The new Constitutions permit the use of the black habit. From time immemorial the Carmelites had worn a habit of undyed wool (*griseus*), which seems to have been an indeterminate shade of greyish brown. In the course of the 14th century the use of a finer wool cloth dyed black had been introduced in the Order. Soreth does not attempt to alter this trend but strikes a compromise, prescribing the color "grey" tending to black, or black. Laybrothers and semi-fratres continued to wear grey habits of undyed wool. Soreth himself mostly wore an undyed habit, and his biographer, John Taye, ascribes this to the fact that in his humility he wished to conform to the usage of laybrothers. On the other hand the undyed habit seems to have been mandatory for the friars of the Observance.

The mitigation of 1432 with regard to abstinence is incorporated in the new legislation.

An important element in Soreth's program of reform is the establishment of monasteries of nuns. This form of religious life was so far lacking to Carmel, and Bl. John keenly felt the want of "a company of virgins and young girls" in the Order of the Queen of Virgins. Moreover, houses of religious women, in which the Carmelite way of life was realized to the full, would be a second arm to his reform. Not that Bl. John necessarily began with a full-blown plan in his mind. His policies were probably inspired and guided by the gradual unfolding of events.

In the Netherlands the equivalent of *pinzocchere, mantellate, beatas*, and the like were the beguines. They made promises of chastity and obedience, recited certain prescribed prayers, and lived in their own houses. The latter were grouped together and formed a walled enclosure, the gates of which were locked in the evening at a certain hour. The beguinage also included a chapel, infirmary, and graveyard. A vicar or curate, frequently a religious, took care of the spiritual needs of the sisters.

Such a beguinage, with the name "ten Elsen," was situated in the Carmelite parish of Guelders. The fact that Cardinal Nicholas of Cusa on apostolic visitation in Germany and the Netherlands, 1451-1452, ordered devout women living in community to adopt an approved rule probably caused the beguines of " ten Elsen " to apply to their Carmelite vicar for admission to the rule of the Order. Soreth, who was presiding at the chapter of the Lower German province, acceded to their request on May 10, 1452. He authorized the prior of Guelders to admit them to profession, to live by the rule and institutes of Carmel. He placed the sisters under obedience to the same prior, who with the consent of the provincial was also to provide them with a religious habit and draw up a way of life for them.

Shortly after, the prior general descended into Italy and Tuscany, where a situation similar to that in Guelders had arisen. In 1450 the Carmine of Florence had collected some of its *pinzocchere* into a community, the "house of our white ladies." On August 15 of that year Donna Innocenza, daughter of Simon d'Arrigo Bartoli and three times a widow; Sarah Lapaccini, also a widow; her daughter Lena; and Anna de Davanzati received the habit of Carmel. By 1452 some crisis (possibly conflict over parochial rights) had arisen in the affairs of the *pinzocchere* of Florence, which determined the friars to obtain papal authorization for them. Whatever the reason, it was sufficient to cause the prior, Bartholomew Masi Soderini, to undertake a journey to Rome, in spite of the dangerous condition of the roads, due to a state of war. He returned safe and sound with the bull of Nicholas V, *Cum nulla*, of October 7, 1452.

This historic document granted to the prior general and provincials of the Carmelite Order the same privileges as the Dominicans and Augustinians with regard to the reception, way of life, admission and protection of religious virgins, widows, beguines and mantellates, who singly or in groups were living or in the future would present themselves under the habit and protection of the Carmelite Order. The bull *Cum nulla* granted the fullest powers to Carmelite superiors to admit women to the Order and may be considered the *magna carta* of Carmelite nuns, sisters, and tertiaries.

It was the prior of Florence who actually journeyed to Rome and brought back the papal bull "for the *pinzocchere* at the desire of the whole convent." The community of Florence also paid all expenses incurred in obtaining the bull (63 *lire*, 4 *soldi*, 6 *denari*). These circumstances, however, need not necessarily lead to the conclusion that Bl. John was unaware of Soderini's initiative, which consequently would be to his exclusive credit. The bull makes no mention of the particular circumstances at Florence, as one would expect, if it had been obtained only for this purpose. Also, it is unlikely that the Holy See at the sole request of a local superior would grant a favor applicable to the whole Order without the knowledge of the superior general. In fact the bull is addressed to the "Most Reverend Lord General of the Order of St. Mary of the Carmelites at Rome." Soreth had been in Tuscany since August and, made aware of the problem in Florence, could have urged or permitted the prior to take steps to secure the papal confirmation he also needed for Guelders. Upon his return from Rome Soderini journeyed to Pistoia in connection with the bull, presumably to consign to Soreth his copy, which hardly could have come as a complete surprise, pleasant or otherwise. A second copy remained in Florence, "the property of the mantellates or beguines of the convent of Florence of the Tuscan province of St. Mary of the Carmelites." In any case Soreth was later to state that he had himself obtained the bull.

At the provincial chapter convened in Prato on November 8, 1452, the prior general placed "our sisters in Florence" in the care of Elijah Goffredi, a French reformed friar of the Mantuan Congregation, who was also appointed reformer of the Florentine friary and *socius* of the provincial. Elijah was reconfirmed as director of the sisters by the chapters of 1453 and 1454.

"The house of the white ladies," if it was the occasion of acquiring the bull, was of short duration. On October 10, 1454, we find Donna Innocenza again attempting to form a community, this time in a house donated by a devout benefactress, Donna Andrea Bornarli. Her companions were two young women, Rosa di Giovanni Filippi and Mattea Chellini, professed the previous year. This foundation endured, though it was not yet a cloistered monastery. In 1480 the prior general, Christopher

27

Martignoni, granted the sisters the scapular, the habit of the Order and symbol of the cloistered life. In 1521 they received the black veil, sign of the obligation to recite the divine office in choir and of capitular rights. It was the end of a long term of development of the monastery of St. Mary of the Angels, which was to become the most important monastery in the Carmelite Order and future home of St. Mary Magdalen de' Pazzi.

But Donna Innocenza's was not the only or earliest Carmelite monastery in Florence. She was preceded in 1453 by Donna Antonia Spadaro, who formed a company of *pinzocchere*, called the Nunziatina after a terra cotta image of the Annunciation, which the sisters placed in the midst of their houses. In 1517 they moved into a single house and undertook the cloister. The Nunziatina has been overshadowed by the more famous monastery of St. Mary of the Angels, but it continued its life of hidden prayer until its suppression in 1786 by Archduke Peter Leopold of Tuscany.

Back in Germany a year later, the prior general wrote to the sisters of Guelders from nearby Mörs, October 14, 1453, confirming their admission to the rule, habit, and profession of the Order, this time by virtue of the privilege "which we have obtained from our Most Holy Lord and Father, Pope Nicholas V." He also prescribed various "conditions and decrees," his first statutes for Carmelite sisters, which unfortunately have not come down to us. It is likely that their form of life resembled that of the sisters of Nieukerk, whose statutes refer to Guelders.

During the following years and the remainder of his generalate Bl. John Soreth took a keen interest in the sisters of the Order and was himself personally involved in the foundation of a number of monasteries deriving from Liège.

It is again from Mörs that we find the prior general writing, on August 15, 1455, this time to the *"sorores inclusae Ordinis"* of Nieukerk, a town between Guelders and Aldekerk in the Dukedom of Guelders. These sisters, apparently originally beguines, had already been living under the Order for some time; Soreth now admits them by virtue of his papal faculties. He appoints Peter van Nieukerk his vicar who is to translate the rule and Constitutions, as far as they apply to the sisters. Access to the cloister (*inclusorium*) is denied to all men, religious or lay. For this reason a parlor is to be built, where the mother of the house (*mater domus*) may receive visitors. The cloistered sisters may never go out; the errands of the community are done by the non-enclosed sisters who wear the white mantle but no capuche (that is, scapular). After they move into the new cloister the sisters are to lead a common life: eat together in the refectory, work in a common work-room and re-create together at fixed hours in fixed places.

Dinant may have been founded before Nieukerk; it was canonically approved by the bishop of Liège, John of Heinsberg, who resigned November 22, 1455. He had given permission for the beguinage or hospital of Sts. John the Evangelist and Mary Magdalen to be transformed into a monastery, on condition that the aged and infirm beguines be supported for life by the Carmelite sisters. In 1459 Soreth obtained papal approval for the establishment. Their life is adequately described by a magistrate of Dinant, writing to the general of the Premonstratensians in 1456 about "certain devout women of the Order and habit of Our Lady of Mount Carmel enclosed in monastic cloister, who continually perform the service of God in contemplation." In 1466 Dinant experienced the vengeful wrath of the Count of Charolais, the future Charles the Bold. The sisters fled the general destruction to Huy and Namur. From Namur they returned to Dinant in 1603.

In 1457 the bishop of Liège granted permission for a monastery of Carmelite sisters, dedicated to the Three Marys. Funds came from money left by a sister of Sister Agnes, a recluse at the Carmelite church. John Soreth himself contributed much to the building of church and convent in this, his favorite city where he returned after his frequent journeyings. The bishop placed the sisters under Soreth, "whose life, morals and conversation in the

Lord we praise." In Soreth's absence the prior of the convent of reformed friars was in charge. The sisters too were of the observance, had no personal property or rents, recited the canonical hours and observed perpetual enclosure. When Charles the Bold took the city in 1468, the sisters took refuge in Maastricht. They soon returned to their ruined monastery and restored it. The sisters of Liège took in young girls as "scholars" to whom they gave instruction and from among whom they recruited novices. In 1575 they erected a separate boarding school which flourished until the French Revolution.

At Huy the sisters fleeing from the destruction of Dinant in 1466 found refuge in an old hospital in the parish of St. Germain. The new foundation was under the jurisdiction of the reformed friars of Liège. The sisters had the right to present a Carmelite friar for pastor; in 1521 they obtained the right from the Holy See to elect a Carmelite confessor. Since this was the prerogative of the prior of Liège, a long-standing quarrel arose. The way of life at Huy resembled that of Liège. Soreth bestowed considerable time and effort on this monastery, begun under such trying conditions. When the troops of Liège again sacked the city in 1467, the sisters stayed put. These and other disasters apparently did not succeed in dampening the recreations. Some nativity plays in the dialect of Liège presented by the sisters of Huy are still extant.

At Namur, the other haven of the refugees from the destruction of Dinant in 1466, a site for a convent was found outside the city walls. In 1468 Bishop Louis de Bourbon canonically approved the foundation and at Huy and Liège appointed Soreth and the prior of Liège as visitators. Ten years later the sisters settled in the hospital of St. Callixtus at Jambes near Namur. During the early difficult years Soreth was often on hand to help.

Not all the sisters who fled to Maastricht from Liège in 1468 were afterwards able to return home. The reduced economic condition of the convent was not equal to supporting the former community. In 1469 Soreth found a place for the remainder of the sisters in an old beguinage at Vilvoorde near Brussels. The new foundation was to depend juridically on the friary at Brussels, as soon as it accepted the reform. The presence of beguines in the establishment, the unsatisfactory financial arrangements for the support of the sisters, were elements that did not make for peaceful existence, and the monastery experienced much litigation. At the death in 1477 of Charles the Bold, who had conceived the plan in the first place, there were threats from patriots to set fire to the convent and drown the confessor. An ancient statue of Our Lady of Consolation was and still is venerated at Vilvoorde, for this of all Soreth's foundations is still in existence.

This statue had been venerated in the beguinage of Our Lady of Consolation and was the gift in 1247 of Sophia, Duchess of Brabant, who had received four statues from her mother, St. Elizabeth of Hungary. The other three Sophia gave to her sister-in-law, Mechtilda, who in turn bestowed one on the Carmelites of Haarlem. "The fair Order of Carmel should rejoice," writes John Lezana, "that of four most precious jewels it should have two." The statue was thought to have escaped the suppression of the Haarlem convent in 1578 and in a miraculous manner to have found its way to Brussels. It does in fact seem to have survived, but to have found asylum instead in the beguinage of Haarlem. When the Carmelite nuns took over the beguinage of Vilvoorde in 1469, they also took charge of its miraculous Virgin. In 1579 during the Calvinist reign of terror the statue was saved by a laysister, Catherine Vayems, who, dressed as a peasant, smuggled it out of the city in a swath of hay on her head. At Mechelen, where the nuns fled, the statue escaped unharmed in the seizure of the city by Olivier van den Tempel in 1580. In 1587 when the *gueux* again sacked Vilvoorde the statue once more remained intact. During the continual wars of the 17th century the nuns several times carried their precious treasure to safety in other cities, Brussels, Antwerp, Mechelen. It consists of a bust of the Virgin holding the Infant on her left arm, is carved from oak and 63 cm. in height. "The features, appropriately colored, have a remarkable expression of tenderness which reassures and consoles."

Outside this circle of Walloon foundations with which Soreth is directly connected, a monastery, dedicated to Our Lady of Jerusalem, was founded in 1466 at Haarlem under the jurisdiction of the local prior. The sisters came from Guelders, or at least had spent a period of training there. The parish had rather stringently limited public functions in the chapel that might be a source of income, so the sisters supported themselves by their own labor, spinning, growing, steeping and combing flax. The sick of the area are visited on request. It is not clear whether all the sisters or only some of them engaged in such visiting, nor consequently whether they were cloistered or not. The fact that they were connected in some way with Guelders and sent sisters to Bruges, both cloistered monasteries, would seem to indicate that they were.

After Soreth's death the monastery of Haarlem gave rise to a new foundation, in 1482, at Rotterdam.

Bruges, in Flanders, owed its monastery of Carmelite nuns to the initiative of the Carmelite Henry d'Inghel. In 1487 he obtained permission from the municipality for the purchase of a site, as well as the consent of the bishop for a foundation. He had choir books copied at Vilvoorde and Gent and brought two sisters from Haarlem to instruct the candidates in the Carmelite way of life. In 1488 the illustrious Carmelite Adrian van den Eechoute from Gent took charge. Nevertheless construction proceeded slowly. The monastery was dedicated to Our Lady of Sion. Confessors and chaplains at first came not from Bruges, which was not reformed until 1510, but mostly from Gent. The library included a life of Bl. John Soreth and his *Expositio paraenetica*, or commentary on the rule. Treasured in the monastery was the Virgin

Blessed John Soreth and his foundations.
School of Liège, 17th century.

Blessed Frances of Amboise with Soreth's constitutions.
School of Liège, 17th century.

painted by the noted artist Gerard David in 1509, today in the Museum of Rouen.

Liège, the fourth of the new nunneries in the Low Countries, had been in existence only two years, when during a visit to the province of Touraine in 1457 John Soreth met the recently widowed young Duchess of Brittany whose reputation for piety was in the mouths of all. After the death of her husband she had resolved not to marry again, thereby upsetting the dynastic plans for her of her father, Louis of Amboise, and King Louis XI. The latter vainly tried every means of persuasion in his not inconsiderable power, not stopping short of an attempt at kidnapping. Frances wanted to enter the convent of Poor Clares she and her husband had founded at Nantes in 1457, but her health failed her. She considered devoting herself to the care of the poor in a hospital. At this point she met the saintly prior general of the Carmelites, and one of those warm and human friendships between saints ensued. Bl. John had no trouble interesting Frances in the sisters he was establishing in the eastern principalities of Belgium. It was decided that she would endow a monastery at Bondon, near Vannes, where there already was a reformed house of friars.

Bl. Frances of Amboise (1427-1485) was the first child of Louis, Lord of Amboise, Viscount of Thouars, and of Mary of Rieux, of noble Breton stock. An ally of Arthur de Richemont, Constable of France and brother of the Duke of Brittany, Louis was involved in a plot against Georges de la Trémoille, favorite of Charles VII, and was condemned to death, later to life imprisonment. The king bestowed his property on La Trémoille. (Nevertheless a sister of Frances, Marguerite, married the son of the Constable, Louis I de La Trémoille, who had been rejected as the husband of Frances by Louis of Amboise. Among their numerous children were Louis II de la Trémoille, " *le chevalier sans reproche,* " slain in battle at Pavia 1525. A daughter, Jeanne, entered Carmel at Bondon with her aunt and later became prioress of Les Couëts.) Marie de Rieu fled Thouars to the protection of Riche-mont.

In 1431 a contract of marriage was made be-tween Frances, aged four, and Peter, the 13 year-old son of John V, Duke of Brittany, at whose court the *"noble et puissante damoiselle,"* now called Madame de Benon, was reared. She was given into the care of the Duchess of Brittany, Jeanne de France, a very devout woman, who no doubt first awakened and shaped the life-long piety of Frances. Jeanne fostered the memory of St. Vincent Ferrer whom she had assisted in his last agony; later Peter and Frances would be among those who requested his canonization. John V died in 1442, and the same year Peter and Frances were married.

In 1450 Peter succeeded his elder brother Fran-cis I as Duke of Brittany. Peter II "the Simple" was not one of the greater dukes of Brittany. He seems to have been a rough and impulsive but withal not unlovable type. On one occasion he beat his wife Frances of Amboise until blood flowed. Frances' piety did not make her less attractive nor blunt her appreciation of fine things. A chronicler describes her at a wedding being led in the dance by the Count of Laval attired in " a gown with golden flowers on a crimson ground edged with sable." A sermon against women's fashions aroused her scruples, and thereafter she dressed more sim-ply. Still her accounts continue to show bills for items like fine cloth, her hairdresser, the upkeep of her greyhounds.

Frances showed a sound grasp of practical affairs and she probably influenced her husband in more than one decision. Duke Francis II, his successor, in 1469 testified that Frances "always concerned herself with the public good and the preservation of the unity of our country and duchy." At his death in 1457 Peter witnessed in his testament to "the long association and companionship in mar-riage which we and our very dear and beloved sis-ter and companion spouse, Frances of Amboise, have shared from our earliest youth, the good and agreeable services of great obedience and humility she has shown us in health and sickness. "

Frances of Amboise bore him no children, but probably not, as pious biographers opine, because of a vow of virginity. Peter left a natural daughter, Joan.

A former Duke of Brittany, John V, had founded the convent of friars at Bondon in 1425. Frances now proposed to add a monastery of Carmelite nuns. In 1460 Frances obtained authorization for the foundation from Pius II. The pope specifies that the sisters, like the friars of Bondon, are to live according to the regular observance and the mitigated rule, recite the choral office according to the Carmelite rite, observe enclosure and renounce possessions. In 1463 nine sisters arrived from Liège. " On November 2, 1463, " a chronicle records, "at 4 o'clock in the afternoon the said sisters arrived at Vannes, accompanied by the Reverend Father John Soreth, who always preceded them to find a place to say Mass for them and give them Communion. When they came to the gate, the gentlemen of the city received them honorably and conducted them to the castle of l'Hermine near Les Lisses. There they stayed until the Feast of St. Thomas the Aposle, when they came out to inspect the convent which was being built. Toward evening they were taken to see the church of St. Peter. They lived in the upper storey of the castle and there performed the divine office and other religious exercises, rising at midnight, accompanied by the holy Duchess." On February 1 the sisters took possession of their new convent, dedicated, like the mother house in Liège, to the Three Marys. As confessor to Bl. Frances, Soreth appointed the former prior of Liège and at the time subprior at Gent, Matthew de Lacroix, who became her first biographer. Arnold Bostius remembers him setting out with Soreth around Epiphany of 1467.

On March 25, 1468, Bl. Frances of Amboise received the habit of Carmel at the hands of Bl. John Soreth. The former duchess insisted on being treated the same as any novice, to the embarassment of the sisters, many of them no doubt simple country girls. Too frequently in those times the class distinctions of secular society continued to determine relationships within religious communities. Some institutions specialized in the left-over daughters of royal and noble families. "We are all sisters wearing the same habit and making the same profession," Frances later taught as prioress. "The rule is not longer for one than for another. ... To consider and be concerned with who is the grandest lady and comes from the noblest and richest family is the doctrine of the devil. " These are strong words for a Frenchwoman in the age of Burgundian splendor.

After a decent interval, two years after her profession, Bl. Frances was elected prioress and remained such for the rest of her life. It was an arrangement little to her liking, and she pleaded with the sisters to be released from the burden.

The conferences of Bl. Frances of Amboise to her communities have come down to us in the form of notes taken by one of the sisters. The range of subject matter is limited by the current spiritual needs of the audience. Frances stresses obedience, silence, and charity, especially in speech. A kindly and humorously despairing patience shines through these admonitions to correct constantly repeated faults.

By one of the curious literary peregrinations of the book trade the psalter of Bl. Frances has ended up in the Pierpont Morgan Library in New York City (ms. 84).

In 1476 Sixtus IV at the request of Duke Francis II bestowed the Benedictine priory of Les Couëts near Nantes on Bl. Frances and her community. The seven nuns who remained were to join the parent abbey of St. Sulpice or become Carmelites. Their religious observance left much to be desired, yet one sympathizes with their adverse reaction to this arrangement made on their behalf. For several years they waged a brave but ineffectual legal battle. In 1480 the sisters remaining at Bondon migrated with papal permission to Les Couëts, and the original foundation was abandoned. The community also obtained privileges guaranteeing that their direction would be confided to reformed friars.

Nevertheless, Bl. Frances always regretted leaving Bondon and hoped to return there one day. After her death this desire was made known to her niece, Anne of Bretagne, daughter of Duke Francis II of Brittany, and at the time wife of Charles VIII. In 1513 Queen Anne, "greatly desiring that the intention and original devout wish of our late and aforesaid aunt be accomplished," gave orders to proceed with the project. A new site not far from the old was chosen. The stones of the old monastery were used to construct the new one. Nevertheless it was not until 1530 that 18 nuns, 2 novices and 1 postulant arrived from Les Couëts to open the monastery of Our Lady of Nazareth. The original arrangement called for one vicar to be elected jointly by both monasteries, but this proved impractical, and the sisters of Nazareth in 1544 received permission from Paul III for their own vicar. A certain coolness developed between the two houses over this incident.

For John Soreth the institution of the sisters was part of his program of the Order. This explains the cloistered nature of their life, for a return to a more retired and recollected existence was one of the features of his observance for the friars. The convents of friars founded during Soreth's time were all of the observance; it was inevitable that the institution of the sisters took the form it did. However in the age of spiritual decline the problem of maintaining the original spirit of the new institution was a serious one.

During Soreth's lifetime there was no problem; the prior general placed the monastery of the Three Marys under his own jurisdiction, an arrangement approved by the general chapter of Aurillac in 1469. At least so the sisters later contended. The province of Touraine claimed its provincial had exercised this right from the start. In 1473 Soreth's successor, Christopher Martignoni, withdrew the sisters from the authority of provincials. After Les Couëts was founded, he gave Bl. Frances the right to choose confessors from any province (1477). In 1483 Sixtus IV placed Les Couëts under the prior general and gave the sisters powers to elect reformed friars as vicars and confessors. The vicar is to be confirmed by the prior general, or if he cannot be reached, by the bishop of Nantes, who is also named the protector of the monastery.

Needless to say, this privilege was vigorously contested over the years. The right of the sisters to choose any friar they wished, even provincials, to serve their needs at times wreaked serious hardships. The privilege, of course, was also used by some to escape the control of superiors. It ended by working the opposite effect than intended. Removed from all control except that of the far-off general, Les Couëts in the 17th century fell into disorders which one prioress of Nazareth calls "the shame of Carmel."

The monasteries deriving from Soreth's influence were united by a uniform body of legislation. He wrote constitutions for the sisters of Liège, now lost. These he no doubt applied to the other foundations in the principality — Dinant, Huy and Namur — and to Vilvoorde in Brabant. Excerpts from the lost constitutions observed at Vilvoorde and Huy show a mutual affinity with those in force in Britany, of which 17th century copies exist. Thus the origin of the latter is also clear; the foundresses of Bondon imported the constitutions of Liège. With regard to the monasteries in the Flemish and Dutch area, Guelders, Haarlem, Rotterdam and Bruges probably followed the constitutions of Nieukerk. Did Soreth use these for Liège? References in the Breton constitutions to beguinages would seem to indicate that this was so.

Credit for the early development of cloistered life in Italy goes to the Mantuan Congregation. The reform provided these early Italian monasteries with uniform legislation and fervent spiritual direction, similar to the foundations of Soreth north of the Alps.

At first the Mantuans showed only cautious reserve with regard to the direction of nuns. In 1469 the chapter of the Congregation stipulated that not even the vicar general but only the chapter of the

Congregation could permit a friar to undertake the direction of nuns, " because of the danger imminent in this matter." These precautions are not due to a lack of interest in the sisters but to the conditions of the times, when misconduct in nunneries was often precisely due to the friars who had the right of entry. The regulation of relations to nuns, however, does not seem to have discouraged their care, for by 1487 at least three monasteries existed under the Congregation. The chapter of that year provided for them and others to be founded in the future. "In order that this may be done in such a manner that a good report may come to the ears of the laity, credit accrue to the Order and the Congregation, and praise be rendered to God through the chastity, integrity, and devotion of the nuns," rules are laid down for their direction. Confessors are assigned for the monasteries in Parma, Reggio Emilia, and Brescia.

Parma, the earliest of the Mantuan nunneries, seems to have originated from a community of *pinzocchere*, who at an unknown date joined the Order. There is evidence in 1465 of " an association of ladies established in the church of St. Mary of Carmel" in Parma. Dedicated to St. Mary Magdalen, this monastery was made illustrious by the presence of Bl. Archangela Girlani (*d.* 1495). Born in Trino, she entered a monastery there, but finding the proximity to her family too distracting, she was persuaded to enter the recently founded Carmel in Parma. Not long after her profession she was elected prioress.

When the time came to make a foundation in Mantua, Archangela was chosen to initiate it as prioress. The new monastery, founded in 1492 through the generosity of Marquis Francis II, his wife Elizabeth d'Est, and his brother Louis Gonzaga, was dedicated to Our Lady of Paradise. To do a good job of building a paradise on earth, one writer puns, "required an archangel in name and deed." Such was Archangela's reputation for holiness among her contemporaries. She is said to have been particularly devoted to the Blessed Trinity. A contemporary and native of Mantua — in fact, he was prior there in

1493 — was Bl. Baptist Spagnoli. No doubt these two saintly Carmelites knew each other.

Another saintly nun is associated with the foundation of the monastery of Reggio Emilia. Blessed Joan Scopelli was born in that city in 1428, the daughter of John and Catherine Scopelli. She was clothed in the Carmelite habit but continued to live at home. After the death of her parents, from 1480 to 1485, she lived with a widow of modest means, who together with her two daughters put herself under Joan's spiritual guidance. In 1485 she opened the monastery of Santa Maria del Popolo, which she had acquired from the general of the Umiliati. The Mantuan friars took over the care of the sisters. Bl. Joan died in 1481. She was greatly devoted to the Blessed Virgin and practised an unusual devotion which she called "Our Lady's Gown" (*camicia*). It consisted in the recitation of 15,000 Hail Marys, interspersed after every 100 Hail Marys with the *Salve Regina*. At the end, the *Ave Maris Stella* or *O Gloriosa Domina* was recited seven times. The community still recited the "Gown" in 1773.

About the year 1486 the monastery of St. Jerome was founded in Brescia by Sister Olma, of that city. At the time the Mantuan Congregation was attempting to detach the friary of Brescia from the province of Venice, and the spiritual jurisdiction over the nuns remained in the balance. In 1490 the sisters indicated their preference to live according to the reform. After the friars of Brescia joined the Mantuan Congregation, the sisters followed suit.

Eleanora of Aragon, duchess of Ferrara, in 1480 brought from Reggio Emilia Sister Dorothea and seven companions to found the monastery of St. Gabriel in Ferrara. The sisters followed the Augustinian rule, but in 1489 the duchess persuaded them to accept the Carmelite rule and the direction of the friars of the convent of St. Paul of the Mantuan Congregation. The following year Master Baptist Paneti received their profession, on which occasion he presented them with his translation of the rule into Italian.

After Bl. Archangela's death a monastery was

founded around 1493 in her native Trino and placed under the care of the Mantuan friars there.

To the two monasteries in Florence the Mantuans around 1508 added a third, dedicated to St. Barnabas. The foundation came about through the efforts of Master David Esau de Girolamis Cerci. The foundress was Sister Anna Cambina (*d.* 1528).

The constitutions of three Mantuan monasteries are known at present. Those of Parma were composed by the nuns's confessor, Thomas di Caravaggio, not later than 1481. Adopted in Mantua, Ferrara, St. Barnabas (Florence), and St. Mary of the Angels (Florence), they exercised a wide influence in Italy, especially through the prestigious St. Mary of the Angels, which in turn later provided legislation for other monasteries. The constitutions of Mantua are a revision by Angelo of Genoa, confessor of the monastery and of the newly appointed prioress, Bl. Archangela Girlani. Angelo had also been confessor of Bl. Joan Scopelli during the last two years of her life. The third set of constitutions derive from an unknown monastery, possibly Reggio Emilia.

These constitutions, based on those of Soreth (1462), reveal fully developed monastic structures, involving choir, cloister, and chapter rights. Manual labor was prescribed, even though the incomes of the monastery did not require it, and was carried on in a common room to the accompaniment of spiritual reading or hymn singing (as in the Sorethian monasteries). In Parma, meditation was also done in common. A striking feature of the Mantuan legislation is the right accorded to the nuns to be represented at the general chapters of the Congregation.

Chapter III

THE SPANISH MONASTERIES
AND SAINT TERESA

In Spain mantellates, *pinzocchere*, beguines — devout women not living in papal cloister — were called *beatas*. After the bull *Cum nulla* (1452) they began to form communities, though not always cloistered nunneries, as in the Netherlands, France, and Italy. The Sorethian reform never penetrated the Iberian peninsula, nor did a movement arise there like that of Mantua; consequently the development of cloistered life was haphazard and slow.

It was especially in Andalusia that communities of sisters formed. Around 1457 in Ecija a group of *beatas* accepted the Carmelite rule and placed itself under the direction of the friars. Foundress and first superior of the convent of Nuestra Señora de los Remedios was Doña Mencía de Jesús. In 1508 at the directive of the provincial, Luke de San Vicente, María Ana de San Sebastián took over the care of a community of *beatas* in Granada. The new *beaterio*, called Our Lady of the Incarnation, was placed under the bishop for lack of a friary in Granada. From the beginning the community was large, soon numbering fifty sisters. In 1513 a Carmelite *beata*, the noble lady Agnes Farfán, founded the convent of the Incarnation in Seville under the provincial of Andalusia, then entered herself, taking the name Agnes of St. Michael. The Incarnation of Antequera began as a convent of Dominican *beatas*, founded in 1517 by Maria Ruiz and Lucy Alvarez. In 1520 they adopted the Carmelite rule and were joined by Mary of the Angels and Elizabeth of Jesus, from Ecija, who were to instruct them in the Carmelite way of life. Maria Ruiz was elected prioress and took the name Mary of the Cross. The monastery of Our Lady of Mount Carmel in Aracena, founded by two Carmelite *beatas*, the De Castilla

Infante sisters, in 1536 appears as an established community with *clausura* under the jurisdiction of the bishop. The convent of the Immaculate Conception in Paterna del Campo was founded in 1537 through the efforts of the friars of Escacena, who seem to have brought sisters from Seville. First prioress was Agnes of Saint Mary.

In the province of Aragon, the Incarnation of Valencia was founded through the generosity of Peter Raymond Dalmau. In 1502 the prior of the Carmen of Valencia, Peter Estaña, accepted the monastery on behalf of the Order and gave the habit to six choir nuns. The foundresses, Frances Estaña and Ofrecina Caldés, became prioress and vicaress respectively. In 1506 the prior general, Peter Terrasse, granted the sisters the right to elect a confessor and two assistants. With the consent of the community the confessor could bestow the black veil (sign of the obligation of choir) without approval of the provincial and grant the habit to *beatas* and *semifratres* for the service of the community. Valencia may have been a cloistered community from the beginning; by 1561 it certainly was. The monastery enjoyed an excellent reputation. St. Thomas of Villanova, archbishop of Valencia, was wont to say, "What an odor of lilies exudes from the walls of this house!" Mother Catherine de Tejeda (*d.* 1542) was esteemed for her holiness by St. Louis Beltrán.

Avila, the oldest *beaterio* in Castile, was founded by Doña Elvira González in 1479. She received the habit from the provincial, Andrew de Avila, and became the first superior. In 1513, under the prioress Beatrix Guiera the convent was moved from cramped quarters in the town to a more quiet and spacious site outside the walls. At the same time a more monastic form of life was introduced. On the other hand, the bigger building eventually housed a populous community beyond its economic resources. In 1526 the prior general Nicholas Audet authorized the prioress and two of the older sisters to leave the convent on certain occasions to seek support. The Incarnation, as the convent was called, welcomed noblewomen with sufficient dowry to support themselves. These *doñas* had spacious suites, were served

43

by maids, and entertained friends and relatives. It may have been for the purpose of limiting the visits of the friars that Doña Beatrix in 1521 obtained from the prior general, Bernardine of Siena, the faculty of choosing a confessor and freedom from the visitation of the provincial. The provincial and other friars were prohibited access to the convent under grave penalties.

Fontiveros, also in the province of Castile, may have been in existence before it became a Carmelite community, dedicated to the Mother of God. In 1521 Bernardine of Siena praises the prioress for her work as foundress and confirms her in office for life, as he does the prioress of Piedrahita, Maria Alvarez de Vergas. This *beaterio*, also dedicated to the Mother of God, had been founded around 1460 by Maria Vergas (*d.* 1515), but only subsequently became Carmelite, presumably under her successor, Maria Alvarez de Vergas. In 1572, when an attempt was made to enforce the cloister at Piedrahita, the sisters testified that "at the time the said monastery was founded, the sisters received the habit only as *beatas* of the Order of Our Lady of Mount Carmel and wore a white veil. The same sisters at the time of foundation and afterwards professed only the three ordinary vows without ever having promised to observe the cloister... and because the sisters of the said convent pronounced their vows and lived in the manner and habit of *beatas* of the said Order, they were accustomed for many years to go out both in quest of alms in the said town and to the homes of others, parents and relatives, to cure their illnesses and remedy their needs."

The heterogeneous nature of observance in the Spanish foundations, the result of their diverse origins, rules out the existence of a single body of legislation. Most of the ten monasteries mentioned above had been founded as *beaterios*, with the exception of Valencia and perhaps also of Seville, Aracena, and Paterna del Campo. By the middle of the sixteenth century the Andalusian foundations had developed into cloistered monasteries. In Castile, Piedrahita and probably also Fontiveros continued to profess themselves *beatas*, that is, simply professed religious without cloister.

A copy of constitutions for Spanish nuns, dating from the end of the fifteenth or the beginning of the sixteenth century, has in fact come down to us. Composed for "a monastery of the Incarnation," it was at once thought to belong to Avila, but a better knowledge of the history of the Order in Spain has shown that there were at least four Incarnations in the period in question. Moreover, whereas Avila did not profess the cloister, these constitutions prescribe the regular observance in its most evolved form, with recitation of the divine office, community life, vows, and cloister. As a matter of fact they show close similarity with the legislation of Brittany and seem to derive from a common source. The influence of Blessed John Soreth may after all not have been wholly wanting in the Carmels of Spain.

It was in the " open " monastery of Avila — and precisely because of that openness — that a great spiritual revival of Carmel took place. There in 1535 Doña Teresa de Ahumada y Cepeda was clothed in the habit of the Order.

The life of St. Teresa, one of the most remarkable women of all time, has been told by herself and has been the subject of innumerable biographies, hence needs no retelling here. Her indefatigable activity as a foundress of contemplative monasteries was preceded by a long period of intense inward struggle, before she herself accepted her contemplative vocation.

Doña Teresa's life in the Incarnation was similar to that of the other wealthy ladies there. She had her rooms, where she could converse with her friends. She was permitted, at times even commanded, to leave the monastery for reasons of health or of the spiritual edification of influential persons, whose desire was law to her superiors. In fact, not long after her entry Teresa became seriously ill and was removed by her father, Don Alonso Sánchez de Cepeda, in order to receive better care, but to no avail. She was returned to the monastery "nothing but bones" and in a state of paralysis which lasted three years. All her life Teresa suffered ill health.

Early in her illness Teresa made the acquaintance of Francisco de Osuna's *Third Spiritual Alphabet* (Toledo, 1527) and began to practice meditation, even arriving at passive forms of prayer, but after her recovery she did not return to these practices, even though she continued to live a devout and exemplary life. Eventually however her confessor, the Dominican Vincent Barrón, persuaded her to resume mental prayer. But now her worldly attachments began to trouble her. "I spent nearly twenty years on that stormy sea, often falling in this way and each time rising again, but to little purpose, as I would only fall once more . . . I can testify that this is one of the most grievous kinds of life which I think can be imagined, for I had neither any joy in God nor any pleasure in the world.

From this impasse Teresa was delivered by several providential occurences. Her resolve was first stirred during Lent of 1554 by the sight of an image of Christ. "It represented Christ sorely wounded; and so conducive was it to devotion that when I looked at it I was deeply moved to see Him thus, so well did it picture what He suffered for us. So great was my distress when I thought how ill I had repaid Him for those wounds that I felt as if my heart were breaking, and I threw myself down beside Him, shedding floods of tears and begging Him to give me strength once for all so that I might not offend Him. . . . I believe I told Him then that I would not rise from that spot until He had granted me what I was beseeching of Him. And I feel sure that this did me good, for from that time onward I began to improve."

About this time too there came into her hands the newly translated *Confessions* of St. Augustine (Salamanca, 1554). "When I got as far as his conversion and read how he heard that voice in the garden (bk. 8, ch. 12), it seemed exactly as if the Lord were speaking in that way to me, or so my heart felt. I remained for a long time dissolved in tears, in great distress and affliction. . . . I believe my soul gained great strength from the Divine Majesty: He must have heard my cries and had compassion on my tears. I began to long to spend more time with Him, and to drive away occasions of sin, for, once they had gone, I would feel a new love for His Majesty. "

Teresa was also fortunate in her current confessor, the young Jesuit Diego de Cetina, who was content to let the Spirit have his way with her. "I began to make many changes in my habits, although my confessor did not press me to do so and in fact seemed to trouble about it all very little. But this moved me the more, for he led me by the way of love for God which brought me, not oppression, as it would if I had not done it out of love, but freedom."

The final step in her complete commitment to God came during a period of illness, when she went to live with Doña Guiomar de Ulloa, a friend who plays a large role in her life. A widow at twenty-five, famous for her beauty and frivolity, Doña Guiomar now devoted her life to piety. She probably got to know Teresa at the Incarnation, where she had a sister and two daughters. The two women became as sisters over the years. On this occasion Teresa remained in Doña Guiomar's house for three years, 1555-1558, and during that time frequented Doña Guiomar's confessor, John de Prádanos, the twenty-six year old rector of the Jesuit college in Avila. "This father began to lead me to greater perfection." He guided her to a solution of the problem that continued to haunt her: what to do about human relationships which did not offend God and even appeared obligatory, yet seemed to form an obstacle to her perfect freedom. "He told me to commend the matter to God for a few days, and to recite the hymn *Veni, Creator,* and I should be enlightened as to which was the better and then, beseeching the Lord that He would help me to please Him in everything, I began the hymn. While I was reciting it, there came to me a transport so sudden that it almost carried me away: I could make no mistake about this, so clear was it. This was the first time that the Lord had granted me the favour of any kind of rapture. I heard these words: 'I will have thee converse now, not with men, but with angels.' This simply amazed me, for my soul was greatly moved and the words were spoken to me in the depths of the spirit. . . .

"The words have come true: never since then have I been able to maintain firm friendship save with people who I believe love God and try to serve Him, nor have I derived comfort from any others or cherished any private affection for them. It has not been in my power to do so; and it has made no difference if the people have been relatives or friends. Unless I know that a person loves God or practices prayer, it is a real cross to me to have to do with him. I really believe this is the absolute truth.

"Since that day I have been courageous enough to give up everything for the sake of God, Who in that moment — for I think it happened in no more than a moment — was pleased to make His servant another person. . . . Blessed forever be God, Who in one moment gave the freedom which, despite all the efforts I had been making for so many years, I had never been able to attain, though sometimes I had done such violence to myself that it badly affected my health."

Solitude and a simple life-style now became indispensable.

"Although in the house where I was living there were many servants of God, and He was well served in it, yet, as it was very needy, we nuns would often leave it for other places where we could live honorably and keep our vows. . . . There were also other disadvantages, such as the excessive comfort which I thought we had, for the house was a large and pleasant one. But this habit of frequently going away (and I was one who did it a great deal) was a serious drawback to me, for there were certain persons, to whom my superiors could refuse nothing, who liked to have me with them, and so, when importuned by these persons, they would order me to go and visit them. So things went on until I was able to be in the convent very little." Teresa considered taking her

The Carmelite monastery of Rotterdam,
as it appeared in the 16th century.

Saint Teresa of Jesus, by an unknown 17th century painter.
Oil painting, Saint Albert Center - Rome

dowry and transferring to another monastery of the Order which was more strictly enclosed and of which she had heard good reports. It was "a long way away" and has been variously thought to be Valencia or even one of the Breton monasteries. In any case, her confessor would not hear of her leaving.

At this time Teresa made the acquaintance of the legendary Franciscan penitent, St. Peter of Alcantara, who seemed to her "to be made of nothing but roots of trees." He was also a friend of Doña Guiomar and as a matter of fact had come to Avila to initiate a reformed friary on property of hers. From St. Peter Teresa learned of his ideal of poverty and no doubt also of the Discalced Franciscan nunnery he had founded.

The growth of Teresa's ideal of reform reached a critical moment in the autumn of 1560. One day a group of friends and relatives were gathered as usual in Teresa's cell, and the conversation turned to the way of life in the monastery. The topic may have come up in connection with the austere life led by the Discalced Franciscan nuns of St. Peter. "Half in jest," writes Teresa's niece, Maria de Ocampo, they began to plan "how to reform the rule observed in that monastery . . . and found monasteries after the manner of hermitages, like the original one kept at the beginning of this rule, which our holy fathers of old founded." St. Teresa's notion of the hermitage "like the original one kept at the beginning of this rule, which our holy fathers of old founded," would have been suggested by the fourteenth century Carmelite classic, *The Institution of the First Monks*, which consequently lies at the basis of her reform, a Spanish translation of which, belonging to the Incarnation of Avila, is at present preserved in the archive of the Order in Rome. To Doña Guiomar, who arrived late, Teresa laughingly explained: "These young ladies were saying a short while ago that we should found a small monastery after the manner of the Discalced nuns of St. Francis." Doña Guiomar volunteered to help as much as she could with so holy a work.

The plan of founding a small cloistered monastery was now put into execution, but in a rather devious manner. Doña Guiomar was commissioned to approach the provincial of Castile, Fray Angel de Salazar, and to propose the foundation as her own idea. He willingly gave his consent, but subsequently withdrew it in the face of the vigorous opposition of the municipal authorities, who feared the addition of another monastery to those already existing in the town—the more so because Teresa, encouraged by St. Peter of Alcantara, proposed founding her monastery without stable income. This meant that the townspeople would be continuously importuned for alms. The viewpoint of the town council was not as unreasonable as it is sometimes made to appear. The proliferation of religious houses in Spain was to become a national economic problem which the Cortes repeatedly sought to remedy, only to be overridden by the Crown. In this case too the town lost its appeal to Madrid.

Denied permission by local authorities, religious and secular, Teresa appealed to the Holy See. Once again Doña Guiomar was represented as taking the initiative, for in this way the problem of the prior permission of religious superiors could be avoided. As a matter of fact, in due course she received apostolic faculties, dated February 7, 1562, to found a monastery under the jurisdiction of the local ordinary.

On August 24, 1562, the unpretentious monastery dedicated to St. Joseph was inaugurated in what had been a private dwelling with the profession of four candidates. Gaspar Daza, as representative of the bishop, Alvaro de Mendoza, received the vows. Teresa was present, but not yet as a member of the community. Early in 1563 the bishop made Teresa prioress. On August 22, the provincial, by now mollified by Teresa, allowed her and three companions to remain in St. Joseph's for one year. At the end of this period Teresa asked the papal nuncio, Alexander Crivelli, permission to be confirmed by the provincial, to transfer definitively from the Incarnation to St. Joseph's.

The new monastery observed the "first" or "primitive" rule, in contrast to the rule "according to the Bull of Mitigation." The primitive rule, however, turned out to be, not that observed on Mount Carmel, but that "in the form drawn up by Fray Hugo, Cardinal of Santa Sabina, and given in the year 1248 (*sic*), in the fifth year of the pontificate of Pope Innocent IV." In spite of this misapprehension, at the time by no means limited to her mind, Teresa intended her foundation to present "a picture, however imperfect, of our Order as it had been in its early days."

Yet St. Joseph's was no hermitage; in fact, it was distinguished by an intimate community spirit. The sisters lived in a close relationship from which all distinctions of class and rank were eliminated. In St. Joseph's there were no lay-sisters, though Teresa admitted them in her later foundations. If she limited her communities to thirteen sisters to avoid financial difficulties and consequent relaxation of poverty and the common life resulting from large numbers, this limitation also had the effect of creating an intimate family atmosphere. A happy innovation that contributed effectively to a close community spirit was the recreation period.

Into this closely-knit community Teresa infused the spirit of solitude proper to the eremitical life. Strict enclosure was imposed. The sisters kept to their rooms as much as possible. Prayer other than liturgical, spiritual reading, and work were carried out in solitude. If her ideal of absolute poverty, community as well as individual, had a Franciscan inspiration, Teresa was delighted to discover later that it was also characteristic of the eremitical and Carmelite life. Austerity, another eremitical element, characterized Teresa's foundation. The sisters wore woolen habits and sandals, their rooms contained only the poorest and barest necessities. Total abstinence from meat was observed.

On February 16 or 17, 1567, the great reforming prior general, John Baptist Rossi, known in Spain by the hispanicized form of his surname, Rubeo, appeared in Avila on apostolic visitation.

Teresa was understandably uneasy. "I was afraid of two things," she candidly admits, " first that the general might be angry with me. ... secondly, that he might make me go back to the convent of the Incarnation." Her fears proved to be groundless. According to Julian of Avila, Teresa's friend and biographer, Rossi challenged the bishop's jurisdiction over St. Joseph's on the grounds that he, Rossi, had not been consulted. The prior general might indeed have challenged the bull of foundation on the grounds that it had been surreptitiously obtained, but he was too enlightened to impede a good work for a juridical technicality.

Apparently all the prior general did was to point out to Teresa that although St. Joseph's was subject to the bishop of Avila, she did not on that account cease to be a Carmelite. First of all, he straightened out the matter of the nuns' profession; after his visit they began to make profession in his name, not in that of the bishop. Secondly, he immediately grasped the significance for the Order of what was going on at St. Joseph's. He took Teresa's work under his immediate jurisdiction and made plans for its propagation. His letters patent of April 27, 1568, authorized her to found an unspecified number of monasteries of the Order in Castile. In other words, as a result of Rossi's initiative what might be called the "Observance of Avila" became the Teresian Reform.

The spiritual direction of her nuns posed a problem. For this work Teresa would need friars cut from the same pattern as they. Here again the prior general came to her aid. His letters patent of August 10, 1567, authorize two foundations of "contemplative Carmelites" in the province of Castile. The story is well-known of Teresa's initiation of her Order of friars by the enlistment of " a friar and a half"—the diminutive John of the Cross and Anthony de Heredia.

Teresa went on to found her many monasteries, but with the expansion of the male branch of the Discalced the movement passed out of her hands. No need to enter here into the sad story of the conflict between the Discalced friars and the supe-

52

riors of the Order. To Teresa the quarrel was " an intolerable kind of feud. " Throughout she counselled proceeding in concert with the prior general. "If we had gone to him about the matter," she wrote to Jerome Gracián at Rossi's death in 1578, "everything would have been smoothed out. God forgive the person who has continually put obstacles in the way; for, though you had little confidence in my suggestion, I could have come to an understanding with your Paternity."

Teresa died before the final break with the Order came about. Both she and John of the Cross lived and died as members of the old Carmel.

Teresa's formula for Carmelite life was eminently successful. Today her daughters number over 13,000 in more than 800 monasteries, the largest body of cloistered women in the Church. By their dedicated lives they have made Carmel, with its ideals of solitude, prayer, and total immersion in God, a household word in the Church. Yet Teresa did not succeed in rallying the whole Order, if that was her intent, to her vision. Her version of Carmelite life, valid as it is, bears the indelible stamp of her forceful genius: it is *Teresian*. She provides her sons and daughters with what was previously lacking in Carmel—an immediate, flesh-and-blood model and founder. They do indeed revert to the primitive sources of the Order, but through her; Teresa has become their "Holy Mother."

Nevertheless, in spite of the cold war that has divided the friars of both branches of Carmel, Teresa, especially through her incomparable writings, has also made her presence felt in the old Carmel—a presence, one hopes, that will continue to grow in a more ecumenical future.

During his canonical visitation of Spain and Portugal, 1566-1567, the prior general, John Baptist Rossi did not neglect the sisters, though he did not manage to visit them all. Ecija, Seville, and Antequera in the province of Andalusia by this time are seen to be cloistered, and so perhaps were the other Andalusian monasteries. At Piedrahita in the Castilian province the sisters wore the white veil and did not observe the cloister. Rossi did not insist that they do. "These nuns have embraced the three vows of religion with fervor," he wrote, "excellent morals prevail among them, they dedicate themselves to divine cult with great diligence and integrally keep the cloister"—that is, they did not leave the convent without permission and for a just cause. The account of the visitation of the Incarnation of Avila paints the same picture as does St. Teresa: overcrowding and poverty, lack of common life, class distinctions among the nuns. Here, as at Piedrahita, the sisters did not feel bound to the cloister. To alleviate the poverty of the house, the greatest problem, Rossi forbade the acceptance of more nuns. As a result, in the next twenty-five years the number of sisters of the black veil was reduced by half.

During the second half of the sixteenth century four more Carmels were added. In the province of Aragon the Incarnation in Valencia had so increased in membership as to necessitate a second foundation in that city, dedicated to St. Anne (1565). Ten years later another Carmel issued from the Incarnation, this time in Onteniente (1575). In Andalusia two benefactors, Francis Alvarez Bohorque and Catalina de Coria, founded the Carmel of the Immaculate Conception in Utrera, 1580. The provincial Diego de Cardenas and the local prior Diego de Coria collaborated in the foundation. In 1594 the sisters left Paterna del Campo and returned to Seville, but not to the Incarnation, whence they had set out, but to a new monastery dedicated to St. Anne.

The Carmelite sisterhood was exported to Portugal by an unspecified monastery in Castile. In 1541 a certain Dona Colaça donated the land for a Carmel in Beja. No doubt she knew the Carmelite friars, present in the town since 1526, and may even have been a *beata* of the Order. Her three daughters, one of them a lady-in-waiting in the court of King John III, joined two Carmelite nuns fetched from Castile to make the foundation, dedicated to Our Lady of Good Hope. Of the three Portuguese sisters, Joan of Christ (prioress), Jeronima of St. Bartholomew, and Louisa of the Holy Spirit, the first is remembered for her natural talents as a musician as well as for her virtues, austere life, and devotion to the Passion of Christ. The monastery soon earned a reputation for observance. When Teutonio de Bragança, good friend and correspondent of St. Teresa, undertook to reform the nuns of his archdiocese of Evora, he applied to this monastery for help.

In 1558, the provincial, John Limpo, sent five sisters from Beja to make a foundation in Lagos (Algarve), and in 1571 three sisters left Beja to open a monastery in Tentúgal.

Chapter IV
TRENT AND THEREAFTER

During the middle half of the 16th century, 1525-1575, the Order was ruled by two outstanding priors general, Nicholas Audet (1524-1562) and John Baptist Rossi (1564-1578), both of them passionately committed to the spiritual renewal of Carmel. Their efforts were hampered north of the Alps and the Pyrenees by the Protestant Reformation and the Wars of Religion in France (1562-1598). In the middle of the period lay the momentous council of Trent (1545-1563), which had important consequences for religious women as well as for the universal Church.

At the time of the council of Trent nuns (*moniales*) were religious women who professed the three solemn vows of religion according to an approved rule. In his constitution *Periculoso* (1298) Boniface VIII had determined that solemn vows implied cloister, but this law was by no means universally observed. Tertiaries (sisters who professed a Third Order rule), not having solemn vows, were not obliged to cloister. Neither necessarily were those who, either out of devotion or by papal indult, made solemn vows along with their profession of a Third Order rule. Even monasteries of nuns in the strict sense which had never since time immemorial observed cloister were considered by theologians and canon lawyers to have a *ius acquisitum* or to be tolerated by authorities.

The fathers of Trent renewed Boniface's *Periculoso* without concerning themselves with particular problems of its application to the varied forms of life observed by religious women at the time (*De regularibus*, sess. 25, ch. 5). As a result the matter of cloister became one of the disputed questions of the day. The generals of the Mendicant Orders opposed introducing the cloister where it had not been specifically promised, though they agreed that it might be well to enforce it in the future. Such was Rossi's answer to a question of the Congregation of the Council in 1565.

Pope Pius V by his constitution *Circa pastoralis*, May 29, 1566, put an end to discussion. Nuns by virtue of their profession were obliged to cloister, whatever the tenor of their rules or whatever immemorial customs they enjoyed. The same applied to tertiaries living in community with solemn vows. Tertiaries without solemn vows (simple vows) were forbidden to receive novices in the future and were so condemned to extinction. In other words in the post-Tridentine church all religious women were to be cloistered. This severe measure must be seen in the context of an age in which immorality in houses of religious women was a serious problem.

Predictably there was opposition to the decree. Sisters who had entered "open" monasteries had done so without any intention of committing themselves to cloister. Even where good will existed, urgent social and economic factors sometimes militated against the imposition of the cloister. Some monasteries, notably in the Republic of Venice, traditionally and expressly existed as a solution for the nobility for disposing of extra daughters. These women bore their lot with the best grace possible; to ask them to undertake a rigorous penitential regime was adding insult to injury. Mendicant communities especially could not survive without the possibility of leaving the monastery to beg or otherwise acquire funds.

Trent had given bishops the power of discretion in determining legitimate reasons for leaving the monastery, which some prelates used quite freely. But Pius V, convinced that the key to reform of feminine institutions was the cloister, was not to be outmaneuvered. His bull, *Decori et honestati*, January 24, 1570, restricted the reasons for leaving the cloister to fire, pestilence, and leprosy. Gregory XIII proved no more accommodating. He appointed apostolic visitators to oversee the enforcement of cloister, a move that panicked lagging superiors into immediate compliance. The *Circa pastoralis* had already attempted to overcome the economic difficulties of monasteries by ordaining that begging could be done by non-professed lay sisters (*conversae*); where these were lacking, professed sisters could be used (par. 5). But this solution contradicted the Tridentine principle that solemn vows implied cloister. Gregory XIII, *Deo sacris virginibus*, December 30, 1572, ordered professed *conversae* back to the monasteries as soon as their support was assured. On the other hand he ordained that the alms collected for the poor of dioceses should be shared with impoverished monasteries. These measures often proved inadequate, but the doors of the monasteries remained closed.

During his visitation of the nuns in Spain Rossi did not insist on cloister where it had not been vowed, in keeping with his opinion expressed to the Congregation of the Council, but on returning to Rome in 1568 and learning of the pope's decision, he revoked all permissions to leave the cloister in Spain. To the chronic economic crisis of the monasteries he applied the ordinance of the council: limiting the population of the monasteries to that able to be supported by their incomes (sess. 25, *De regularibus*, ch. 3).

After its origin in the 15th century, cloistered Carmel in the 16th century experienced a time of early growth.

The province of Aragon added a second monastery in Valencia (St. Anne, 1567) and another in Onteniente (1575). In 1580 Andalusia made a foundation in Utrera and in 1564 one in Osuna. In 1594 the community of Paterna returned to Seville, but not to the Incarnation, whence it had originated; instead it made a second Sevillan foundation under the title of St. Anne. At the time of the Discalced secession (1593), the Order possessed thirty-two Teresian monasteries.

The rise of Calvinism marked the end of the monasteries in the northern provinces of the Low Countries at Rotterdam (1572) and Haarlem (1578). Nieukerk too ceased to exist in 1590, and Vilvoorde was damaged by fire (1578). Rossi's interest in the

Order in the impenetrable north included correspondence with the monastery in Bruges. "He (Matthew de Lalande)," the prior general wrote on December 26, 1577, "wrote me many favorable things, praising your way of life, manners, peace and tranquillity, religious fervor, divine cult, excellent reputation among the people; he admired your observance of poverty."

The losses in these regions were not recouped with new foundations. Given the times, this is hardly suprising. The permission which some of these monasteries obtained from the Holy See or the prior general to elect their own vicars, or chaplains, eventually led to much litigation with the provinces. St. Teresa eliminated the offfice of vicar which included authority over internal affairs of the monasteries, and insisted on freedom of choice of confessors.

From 1503 the Carmelites of Cologne were confessors at a beguinage founded in the Butgasse, 1304. In 1549 the prior, Caspar Doroler, composed a rule or statutes according to which three vows were taken. The beguines, or sisters, attended weekday Mass in the friary church: on Sunday they frequented the parish church of St. Maurice. In 1565 Rossi admitted them to the habit of the Order and vows at the hands of the provincial, John Mayer, thus constituting them tertiaries regular of the Carmelite Order. They did not evolve into cloistered nuns until a century later.

In the course of the century the Mantuan Congregation doubled the number of its monasteries. Sutri was founded in 1515. Still in existence today, this monastery was privileged to be given retreats by St. Paul of the Cross, founder of the Passionists. The friary at Vinovo belonging to the province of Lombardy passed to the Congregation in 1517, after which date the founding of the nunnery must be placed. During hostilities between Savoy and Mantua, Duke Charles Emmanuel I in 1616 ordered the friary to be returned to the province. The nunnery does not seem to have survived this change. In 1525 sisters from Brescia helped initiate a foundation in Albino. In 1537 the Augustinian monastery of St.

Lucy in Ferrara took the Carmelite rule under the Mantuan Congregation. A third monastery of the Congregation in Ferrara came about in 1542 when a group of *convertite*, whom Anthony Ricci of Novellara had converted from a life of sin, decided to initiate a cloistered life. A similar case occurred in Bologna, where a number of fallen women, converted by the Lenten sermons of John Baptist Frumenti of Milan, took the Carmelite habit in 1561. Two nuns came from Ferrara to initiate them into cloistered living when they were aggregated to the Congregation in 1582.

The Mantuan Congregation was undoubtedly responsible for the most flourishing growth of Carmelite nuns in Italy, but monasteries also rose in other provinces there. In Naples the distinguished monastery of the Holy Cross of Lucca was founded in 1534 by the pious Ippolito Giunta, a native of Mantua, but at the time a member of the Carmine Maggiore. The foundation was made possible by the munificence of Andrew Sbarra and his wife Cremona Spinelli, citizens of Lucca.

Cremona herself took the habit in the monastery she helped found. The great reforming legislator of the Order himself, Nicholas Audet, drew up constitutions and statutes (1538); the former however are only a cento of the more general principles of the rule of St. Clara. The prior general placed the monastery directly under his own jurisdiction and imposed cloister. Rossi also visited the monastery and left statutes and ordinances (1563). The prince of Cellamare, who had four daughters in the monastery, lavishly embellished it and its chapel (1588). In the course of the 16th century the Holy Cross of Lucca gave rise to monasteries in Putignano (1552) and Castellamare (1560).

In Sicily the Order acquired two monasteries in Palermo. In 1531 the friary there won a ten year legal battle with Sister Sigismonda Xarrat, Poor Clare, over the possession of a former hospital, but ceded it to her on condition that she establish a Carmelite monastery. She complied and became first prioress of St. Anthony at Porta Termini. The monastery had a brief and troubled existence. The prior general, John Stephen Chizzola, suppressed it in 1597, when it had not yet accepted cloister.

The passage of the hospital of St. Anthony to the Order had required the consent, among others, of the prioress of the monastery of St. Lucy of Valverde, the other Carmelite monastery in Palermo. The Congregation of St. Mary of Valverde, said to have had its origins in Belgium in the Middle Ages, after its demise in 1412 contributed several monasteries to Carmel. Besides the monastery of St. Lucy of Valverde in Palermo, which absorbed the community of St. Anthony at its suppression, houses of the congregation in Messina (St. Catherine's) and Castelvetere on the continent (St. Peter and Paul) at an unknown date accepted the Carmelite rule. Even then they maintained a sort of independent federation and owed allegiance to a " *provincialessa.* "

In the province of Lombardy there was a monastery in Milan, but around 1567 it was suppressed by the archbishop. Nuovi was suppressed by Caffardi in 1578 for failure to introduce the cloister. Pontecurone also got into trouble over the cloister, when the minions of the bishop of Tortona came upon Fra Theodore of Piacenza and a companion, Angelus, leaving the monastery early in the morning, after spending the night in a guest house within the monastery precincts (1574). Submitted to torture, Fra Theodore was shown to be innocent of any dishonest actions: nonetheless he was punished for entering the monastery grounds.

St. Mary of the Angels in Pavia was founded around the beginning of the century. In the 17th century the monastery had the benefit of the spiritual ministrations of Dominic of St. Mary, reformer of the province of Piedmont.

There is some doubt whether the Lombardy province ever had a monastery in Cremona.

Our Lady of Hope in Venice was not a cloistered monastery but a group of tertiaries regular with vows, who may perhaps be traced to a confraternity of *laudesi,* or hymn-singers, known to be in existence in 1300. They survived Chizzola's prohibition in 1593 to accept new candidates.

Thus at the end of the century there were twenty-three monasteries in Italy. The Order took a hard knock, May 28, 1599, when Clement VIII withdrew them from its jurisdiction and put them in the care of the bishops. The pope states no reason for his *motu proprio*, but it was no doubt intended as a reforming action to alleviate moral conditions in the monasteries, which in various parts of Italy were a source of grave concern. In the case of the Carmelite nunneries at least it was a needless precaution.

The prior general, John Baptist Caffardi, who had added an unprecedented chapter on the charge of nuns to the friars' constitutions (1586), also drew up constitutions for all Carmelite nuns: *Ordinazioni per le monache carmelitane* (Firenze, Francesco Tossi, 1582). If these ordinances, of which no copy has been found, are the same as the ms. *Constitutioni* preserved in the Holy Cross of Lucca, they were an adaptation of the friars' constitutions to the nuns. Caffardi thus confirms the principle established in the beginning by Bl. John Soreth: the profession of the brothers and sisters of Our Lady of Mt. Carmel is one and the same, and the regulation guiding their lives need vary only as dictated by differences of sex.

The cloistered Carmelite nun of the 16th century realized in a special way the contemplative ideal of the Order. After Trent all nuns were cloistered, but this style of life particularly suited Carmel's vocation to prayer, solitude, silence, and penitence. The prayer of the Carmelite nuns still centered around the liturgy, the Eucharist and the Hours, which were solemnized in chant, but in Italy in the Constitutions of the Mantuan nuns and in those of Caffardi private interiorized prayer in the form of meditation made its appearance, bringing with it a simplification of the performance of the liturgy. St. Teresa ordered the whole office recited without chant, to allow more time for meditation, a novelty of which Rossi strongly disapproved.

The Carmelite nun also revived another feature of the rule: manual labor. In the Carmels of the old Order work was done in common to the accompaniment of spiritual reading, hymn singing, devout colloquies, nor was a time for reasonable recreation excluded.

The Carmelite nun admirably personified and practiced the Order's distinctive devotion to Mary. Bl. John Soreth's eagerness to promote the Carmelite sisterhood was inspired by the consideration that our Lady lacked the counterpart to the Carmelite friar. Mary's purity and virginity, Marian characteristics specially dear to the Order, were most aptly witnessed to by the Carmelite nun who also very fittingly wore the white mantle, the special symbol of these virtues. Monasteries were often dedicated to the mysteries of the Redemption in which Mary played a particular role.

The nuns reflected in their lives the apostolic dimension of the Carmelite vocation. The contemplative life is by nature apostolic, for anyone who claims to love God and hates his neighbor is a liar. The cloistered nun prays and sacrifices on behalf of embattled humanity. In the monastery of St. Mary of the Angels in Florence Sister Mary Magdalen de' Pazzi was deeply concerned about a contemporary problem, the reform of the church.

Italy at this time produced one of the greatest saints of the Order and one of its most exalted mystics. St. Mary Magdalen de' Pazzi was born of the noble Florentine family of the Pazzi and was baptised Catherine on April 2, 1566, in the baptistery of the Duomo, the " *bel San Giovanni* " of Dante, with its exquisite bronze doors by Ghiberti. She was educated by the Cavaleresse of Malta. Even as a girl she was attracted to prayer, solitude and penance. She had a deep devotion to the Eucharist and made her first Communion at the age of ten. Shortly thereafter she made a vow of virginity. She was directed by the Jesuits whose church in the Via de' Martelli the Pazzis attended. When she was nine, Father Andrew Rossi taught her to meditate, using the recently published *Instruction and Admonitions for Meditating the Passion of Christ* by Caspar Luarte, S.J. She brought her little book with her when she entered the Carmelite monastery, where it is still preserved. The accounts of her later mystical experiences show that she never wholly abandoned these girlhood habits of prayer. Her reading included the gospels, " which always gave her more pleasure than any other book," Louis de Granada, Fulvio Androzzi, S.J., and the *Soliloquies* of pseudo-Augustine.

In 1583 Catherine was received as a novice in the monastery of St. Mary of the Angels in Florence, taking the name of Sister Mary Magdalen. Her profession had to be anticipated due to illness, a fever accompanied by violent coughing, which placed her life in danger. The sudden cure was followed by a state of ectasy which lasted forty days. In that state the infirmarian saw that "her face was most beautiful, her skin rosy. ... She did not seem to be the person illness had made thin and deathly pale." For forty days every morning after Mass Sister Mary Magdalen fell into an ecstasy lasting two hours. At other times she experienced " excesses of love. " In the morning ectasies she remained rigid and motionless; at other times she moved gracefully about the room, following the course of her vision in pantomine. When her visions concerned some sorrowful theme, she perspired freely and uttered cries and groans "capable of moving stones to pity." The love of God, the ingratitude of men, judgment, religious life, the Blessed Virgin, the saints are the subjects of her ecstasies. At times a labyrinthine symbolism is evolved; at other times the visions concern abstruse and impenetrable mysteries. "I saw God all glorious in himself," she states of her vision of June 25, 1584. "I remained in this consideration about an hour, in so far as I could judge when I returned to myself, but what I tasted in that abstraction of mind I could not say, since I could not understand what was shown to me. " But her mysticism is by no means abstract; her revelations come to her through an intimate relationship with Christ. In most cases the saint has hardly received Holy Communion when Jesus appears to her in bodily form. " After Communion I saw Jesus all beautiful. He caressed me lovingly and gave my soul a kiss of holy peace." "I seemed to see Jesus all loving at the right hand of the Father, and his

Saint Mary Magdalen de' Pazzi.

The chapel of the monastery
of Saint Mary Magdalen de' Pazzi, Careggi - Italy.
Photo by Riccardo Palazzi.

eyes were so beautiful, I could never describe their beauty." Jesus then goes on to teach her some truth, or the entire "consideration" is taken up with loving union with her divine Bridegroom.

Sister Mary Magdalen's mystical experiences, accompanied by striking external phenomena, continued into the year 1585. The iron curtain of material reality that hides the world of the spirit seemed to take on a gossamer transparency. The periods of community prayer—Mass, divine office, meditation—invariably triggered an "excess of mind," but even at other times—in the refectory, during recreation, in the laundry, in bed—she would fall into trances lasting for hours. On May 2, 1585, at the time the ecstasies were most frequent, the mistress of novices, Mother Evangelista del Giocondo, wrote: "For some time now the experiences of this blessed soul are so continual and frequent that we can hardly find a free moment to speak to her, as she is constantly in a state of elevation of mind." Beginning on the afternoon of Holy Thursday, April 19, 1585, Sister Mary Magdalen entered into an ecstasy which lasted twenty-six hours. She passed from room to room of the monastery, re-enacting the sufferings of Christ. "She did not seem to walk, but rather to be carried, such was the lightness and speed of her step." At the crucifixion she stood for an hour and a half with arms extended. From May 7-9 she engaged in three colloquies with each of the persons of the Blessed Trinity. The colloquy with the Father lasted twenty-four hours, beginning on the evening of May 8. When she spoke in the person of the Father, it was " with majesty and grandeur." Her part was delivered in "a humble and submissive manner." At one point, apparently wrapt into heaven, " she began to circle the room in a dance, making curtsies and steps with such dexterity and grace that she seemed to be, not a creature, but an angel from heaven." Pentecost, 1585, marked the climax of this period. For eight days, from June 8-16, except for a few hours daily, Sister Mary Magdalen was in a continual trance. Seven times, at Tierce, she received the Holy Spirit under various forms. In dialogues with the Holy Trinity she received high intelligences regarding the mystery of God and experienced in her person the meaning of divine union.

This time of spiritual consolations was followed by " the lion's den, " a five-year period of " the greatest trial and affliction of spirit, " beginning Trinity Sunday, June 16, 1585. Gone was the sense of joy in God's presence. Her whole life seemed a mistake and a trick of the devil. She despaired of salvation. She was severely tempted against chastity. She underwent doubts about her vocation. She still occasionally experienced ecstasies, but they brought little comfort and at times were very painful. A child of the sixteenth century, the classic age of demonology, the saint felt that she had been abandoned to the power of the devil. Evil spirits caused her to fall down stairs, beat her, bit her, seemed to be sawing her limb from limb. Their cries rang continually in her ears, so that she seemed to be blaspheming rather than reciting the psalms. She was tempted to run away from the monastery, to commit suicide.

At the same time Jesus was urging her to reform the Church and her own community. A dozen letters exist today, dating from July 25 to September 4, 1586, dictated by the saint in ecstasy and directed to Pope Sixtus V, the cardinals of the Roman Curia, Cardinal Alessandro de' Medici, archbishop of Florence, and to the superiors in Florence of the religious Orders destined to assist in reform: the Jesuits, Dominicans and Minims. These letters, to quote one authority, "compare favorably for feeling and content with the best of St. Catherine of Siena. " It is doubtful whether they reached their destinations, though the addressees living in Florence probably came to know their contents. The saint also wrote privately on the theme of reform to her former confessor, Peter Blanca S.J., a Sister Veronica of Corbona and St. Catherine de' Ricci. The latter's cautious reply, advising her Carmelite sister to consult her spiritual director, is still preserved in the archive of St. Mary of the Angels. Saint Mary Magdalen was also influential in bringing about a greater austerity in the lives of the sisters, changes which were incorporated in the constitutions of the monastery of 1610. Thus the monastery of St. Mary of the Angels of Florence considers itself a distinct expression of the Carmelite ideal.

On the feast of Pentecost, June 10, 1590, in a joyous vision of the saints, Sister Mary Magdalen was freed from "the lions' den." From this time forward, her ecstasies occur less frequently. Often she had requested of God the cessation of the embarassing mystical gift which set her apart from others. Yet she did not remain entirely free of them. During Holy Week of 1592 she again experienced the Passion, this time more painfully than in 1585. On May 3 of the same year occurred the seizure during which, overwhelmed by the thought that God was not loved, she ran about the house ringing the bells, summoning all to love Love. "O Love," she cried, "you make me die and yet I live." Her ecstasies only ceased with her last illness, beginning in 1604.

But if Sister Mary Magdalen de' Pazzi was canonized, it was not for her ecstasies, but for perfection of love, manifested in fidelity to daily duty and sincere dedication to the needs of others. As in her girlhood, she liked to help with household chores. She rose early to light the fire in the kitchen or laundry and spent hours cooking and washing. She was devoted to the aged and infirm; she would have dearly loved to be infirmarian. From 1595 to 1598 she was in charge of the junior professed. In 1598 she was elected novice mistress; in 1604, sub-prioress.

It is in her continued relations with her family and the world outside that St. Mary Magdalen becomes most real and human. The score of her personal letters that remain give the impression that the saint was a frequent correspondent and encourage the hope that a continued search may unearth more. They are addressed to her family, other religious and old friends among the Cavaleresse of San Giovannino. With her father and her brother Geri, she is the nun of the family, reminding them of their religious duties. When she inquires about her nephew Paul, who she hears was ailing, when she asks Geri to send her a bit of nutmeg, the misty image of the exalted mystic suddenly comes into sharper focus.

Worthy of note is the saint's relationship to Maria de' Medici, daughter of Duke Francesco. The ladies of the Florentine court frequented the convent, sometimes availing themselves of their privilege in canon law of entering the cloister. On Epiphany each year Maria de' Medici joined the nuns in a game of picking the name of a saint as a patron for the coming year. After Maria departed for France to become the wife of Henry IV, Sister Mary Magdalen picked a saint for her (John the Baptist) and wrote to tell her the outcome. At the news of the birth of the Dauphin she had the novices sing a *Te Deum*. It was her custom to offer Saturday to the Blessed Virgin for the queen.

Another friend and visitor was Blessed Ippolito Gallantini, the devoted lay catechist of Florence. The saint listened with interest to his accounts of his work, which inspired her with renewed enthusiasm in the service of God.

In 1604 Sister Mary Magdalen took to her bed with the illness that was to be her last. For some time she had been suffering hemorrhages, fever, coughing spells. Violent headaches accompanied her other symptoms, and she could not partake of much-needed nourishment. "In the home of charity," she wryly observed, "I am dying of hunger." In an age when bodies were worn out at forty, her teeth gave out, and severe toothaches added to her pains. She no longer experienced the mystic flights that lifted her above sensations of pleasure and pain. There remained only suffering and with this she was content. "To suffer, not to die," is the motto attributed to St. Mary Magdalen de' Pazzi. If she did not actually utter these words, they express her spirit. "All the wonder," writes one modern biographer, "all the sublimity of her last years on earth consist in her invincible patience, her perfect serenity, her longing to suffer." She died on May 25, 1607. Her last words admirably sum up the continuous act of praise which was her life: "*Benedictus Deus*—Blessed be God!"

While in ecstasy St. Mary Magdalen often described her visions aloud and gave utterance to reflections on the spiritual life. Her sisters copied down her words, adding descriptions of her actions and outward aspect. This compilation in four manuscript volumes constitutes her "works" and at the same time is her biography. Obviously we have here not a systematic treatise on mystical theology, but "the story of a soul." Its central theme is Jesus Christ, mystery of God and salvation of mankind, whose activity is seen in close relationship to that of the Holy Spirit. Other themes to which the saint often returns are the mystery of the church and religious life. St. Mary Magdalen's doctrine is enshrined in rich symbolism and striking mystical experience. It still lies in the current of the Middle Ages, while presaging the dawning period of the Baroque.

Chapter V

THE VINE OF CARMEL BLOSSOMS

The 17th century was marked by a great renaissance of Catholic life, ushered in by the council of Trent. The papacy, which in the past had often been a hindrance to reform, now led and coordinated the vast energy of Catholic religious fervor. Whereas reforming generals like Bl. John Soreth, Nicholas Audet, and John Baptist Rossi had to rely on personal spiritual resources, the new generals had only to implement the directives of a revitalized papacy.

Pope Clement VIII (1592-1605) particularly interested himself in the reform of religious and drew up a program designed especially to eliminate private property and to encourage prayer. He urged the practice of methodical meditation, then first making its debut in religious circles. Clement himself personally visitated the religious houses of Rome, among them the Carmelite convent of Santa Maria in Traspontina. To introduce the Clementine decrees in the Order, the Carmelites providentially had another outstanding prior general, Henry Silvio (1598-1612), whose thorough-going visitation of the entire Order started it effectively on the path of spiritual renewal.

North of the Alps reform originated in the province of Touraine and spread throughout France, Belgium, Germany, and (partially) Poland. In Italy not all provinces accepted reform, but movements arose in Piedmont, Naples (Santa Maria della Vita), and Sicily (Monte Santo and Santa Maria della Scala del Paradiso). On the Iberian peninsula only a few individual convents were persuaded to follow the new ways.

The general chapter of 1645 united all reforms into one, called the Stricter Observance, and ordered constitutions to be drawn up, actually printed in Paris in 1646. These emphasized the traditional Carmelite values of solitude, prayer, and absolute poverty, or the perfect common life. It was this last feature of reform which caused many provinces to hesitate. An approved custom allowed religious to retain money for personal needs, provided it was kept in a common deposit box, to be dispensed by the community bursar. Many exemplary religious, Carmelite and otherwise, lived under this system, but it was open to abuse and militated against the common life. In theory it was only tolerated until the perfect observance of poverty could be introduced.

Through the Stricter Observance especially the Carmelites participated in the fervor of the Catholic Reformation at every level. The Order was led back to the source of its being and made consciously aware of its vocation to prayer. It produced an abundant and significant spiritual literature, the record of the religious experience of its choicest spirits. The Marian element of Carmelite spirituality was stressed, especially through the scapular confraternity. The apostolate became interiorized and charged with new zeal. Even materially the Order prospered: in spite of wars and pestilence its numbers grew, its convents and churches were embellished or rebuilt in the new style.

In 1600 there existed less than fifty cloistered Carmelite monasteries, not as many as there are today. In 1750 the Order numbered over a hundred. The fervid Baroque spirituality, its mysticism, is nowhere more evident than in the monasteries. New foundations were generally made under the aegis of reform. The effect of the Stricter Observance on existing monasteries remains to be investigated. It would seem that the pattern more or less followed that of the friars.

In 1653 the prior general John Anthony Filippini drew up constitutions for Carmelite nuns which were approved by the general chapter of 1680 and published the same year in Venice. Few monasteries however showed any inclination to adopt them.

In Italy growth was particularly marked in the Kingdom of Naples, where Carmelite nunneries had been few, and in the Venetian Republic, where they had been wholly lacking. In many cases monasteries grew out of that peculiarly Italian institution, the *conservatorio*. Of various kinds, the conservatories that concern us here were houses of religious women without cloister or vows which provided an education for girls, especially with a view to recruitment for religious life. Such conservatories corresponded to the needs of the upper middle class which aspired to a good education but was not always eligible for admission to the monasteries reserved for the nobility. Conservatories were easier to found, because the lack of cloister and solemn vows made the sisters' commitment less irrevocable and consequently eased the economic requirements for papal cloister and the consent of the municipality for foundation.

A noteworthy example of such Carmelite conservatories is found in the numerous foundations of Seraphina of God, which were later organized into the Congregation of the Most Holy Savior. Though Carmelite, Seraphina's conservatories were affiliated with neither Carmelite Order, though the old Order subsequently took her under its wing and in the 18th century promoted her canonization. The present Carmelite monastery of Fisciano was originally one of Seraphina's conservatories. (See the appendix on the Congregation of the Most Holy Savior.)

St. Mary of the Angels in Florence, which attracted the daughters of the leading families of that great city, was the Order's most important nunnery in Italy, although it had passed under the jurisdiction of the archbishop in 1520 and had little to do with the superiors of the Order. Made illustrious by the presence of St. Mary Magdalen de' Pazzi, the monastery greatly influenced the other Carmelite nunneries of Italy. Its constitutions, revised in accordance with the saint's suggestions (Florence, 1611), were accepted or imitated in other Carmels.

By 1624 the old and decrepit premises no longer sufficed for the eighty nuns who composed the community. That year Pope Urban VIII gave them the imposing Cistercian abbey in the Piazza Savonarola, Borgo Pinti, with its beautiful church adorned with paintings by Botticelli, Perugino, Ghirlandaio, and other masters.

The interest of Urban VIII, formerly Maffei Barberini of Florence, in the monastery may be explained in part by the presence there of his nieces, Innocenza of the Incarnation (1559-1666) and Grace of the Blessed Sacrament (1607-1665). It was this pope who on May 8, 1626, beatified Sr. Mary Magdalen de' Pazzi. A measure of the isolation of the monastery from the Order may be had from the fact that the brief of beatification did not even mention that Mary Magdalen was a Carmelite, and that the ceremonies held in Rome for the occasion occurred in the Church of St. John of the Florentines instead of Traspontina, only a stone's throw away. A special trip to Florence by the prior general, Gregory Canal, helped to put the Order into the picture. A brief of Urban on April 23, 1627, extended the office and Mass of Bl. Mary Magdalen to the Carmelite Order, since she was a member. There was greater cooperation between the monastery and the Order at the saint's canonization in 1669. The Order contributed 22,000 *scudi* toward defraying the expenses of this event, with the result that the general chapter due to be held in 1672 had to be called off for lack of funds.

After the death of St. Mary Magdalen religious fervor continued unabated. Of the saint's contemporaries, her novice mistress and prioress, Evangelista Del Giocondo (1534-1625) and her girlhood companion and tireless amanuensis, Pacifica Del Tovaglia (1566-1627), long outlived her and carried forward the memory and reality of her holiness. Many of the saint's novices, it need hardly be said, did honor to her training: Mary Sommai (1580-1615), Catherine Angelica Ximénez (d. 1627), Mary Grace Pazzi (1587-1656).

Among the outstanding figures of our period was Sr. Minima of St. Philip Neri Strozzi (1617-1672). Left an orphan at nine years of age, she was reared by her maternal grandmother Ginevra Martellini in the house of her uncles. Another uncle, the Oratorian Peter Bini directed her youthful piety, but when her family objected to the public practices of penance he imposed, the archbishop of Florence Peter Niccolini substituted him with the Carmelite Albert Leoni. It was no doubt due to his influence that she decided to enter the monastery of St. Mary of the Angels (1634). Much of her life was occupied with the responsible offices of prioress and novice mistress. Besides maxims, conferences and letters published in her biographies she wrote *Istruttioni spirituali* (Perugia, 1671).

One of Sr. Minima's notable subjects and her biographer was Serafica Orlandini (1650-1727). She was greatly attached to her only brother, more so after the death of her parents, but when he also died, she took it as a sign that God was calling her to himself. Lives of St. Teresa and Mary Magdalen de' Pazzi inclined her to Carmel, but left her undecided which Order to choose. Eventually she entered the monastery of St. Mary of the Angels (1667), renouncing without a qualm the wealth to which she was sole heiress. By her holiness of life, practical sense, and qualities of leadership she contributed as few others to the spiritual and material welfare of the community. For many years she served as *camerlenga*, or bursar, and placed the monastery on a secure financial basis in spite of the frequently difficult times. Grand Duke Cosimo III learned to appreciate her qualities in the course of the building of a chapel in honor of St. Mary Magdalen de' Pazzi, which he commissioned in the monastery church. Elected prioress eight times, she served in this capacity for twenty-one years. She re-introduced perpetual adoration of the Blessed Sacrament, for some reason discontinued since the days of the saint, and added a year of novitiate to the period of formation of candidates. In times when the most ferocious penances were practised she advised mortification of the will. Prayer for her was above all doing the will of the Father as expressed in the Lord's Prayer. She stressed the essential Christian qualities of meekness and charity.

Among Sr. Orlandini's literary remains are a revised edition of Puccini's life of St Mary Magdalen de' Pazzi (Lucca, 1716) and of Strozzi's life of Sr. Minima (Florence, 1737). She had previously written a *Brief Sketch of the Life of Sr. M. Minima* (Lucca, 1717) with an appendix of Minima's spiritual maxims. She also wrote a volume of collected lives of the sisters of St. Mary's monastery and a life of Gesualda of St. Joseph Gianni (1654-1725) which remained unpublished.

Biographer in turn of Serafica and of her eight companions in the novitiate was Sr. Teresa Mary Magdalen Trenta (1670-1740). Daughter of a distinguished family of Lucca, she is the subject of an interesting romantic story. When King Frederick IV of Denmark, then heir apparent, visited Lucca in 1692, he met Mary Magdalen at a ball in his honor and was evidently much taken with her. After his return to Denmark and her entry into the monastery of St. Mary's in Florence, he sent her royal gifts and on his second visit to Italy in 1708 did not fail to visit her on March 21. One would like to think that their long conversation concerned something other than an attempt on the part of the nun to convert the king to Catholicism, as pious biographers assert. In the course of her long life Teresa served as novice mistress and prioress. She is credited with an anonymous *Ristretto della vita di Santa Maria Maddalena de' Pazzi*, printed in Lucca by Salvatore and Giovanni Domenico Marascandoli. Her lives of Serafica Orlandini and companions remained unpublished.

St. Mary's gave rise to the illustrious monastery of the Incarnation in Rome, requested, or ordered, by Urban VIII. The prioress of St. Mary's, Mary Grace Pazzi, niece of the Florentine saint, was chosen to head the new community which included, besides the two papal nieces Innocenza and Grace, six other nuns, among them the newly professed Minima of St. Philip Neri. The pope settled the Carmelites near at hand to the Quirinal, at Quattro Fontane in the Strada Pia. The brief of foundation is dated August 1, 1639. When Mary Grace and three others returned to Florence, Sr. Innocenza became prioress. Urban's sister-in-law, mother of his two nieces, Donna Constance Barberini (1575-1644), also joined the community, but was allowed to make profession only on her deathbed. By 1654 the community numbered twenty-four. Urban had expressly specified that only daughters of nobility be admitted. Innocenza drew up *Constitutions* (Rome, 1658), using as her sources the constitutions of the Carmelites, Jesuits and Visitandines. At the same time *Essercitii spirituali* (Rome, 1658) practised in the monastery were published. For obvious reasons the monastery and its nuns were called "the Barberine."

Sr. Innocenza absented herself briefly from Rome in order to found the monastery of Mount Tabor in nearby Monterotondo. Among its early members were Serafina of the Holy Spirit (*d.* 1722) who accompanied the foundress as an *educanda*, still too young to take vows, and Mary Magdalen of the Cross (*d.* 1669). *Instruttioni* published for this monastery in Rome, 1668, followed the general lines of the constitutions of the Roman motherhouse.

The Barberine also founded the monastery of Mount Carmel at Vetralla in the diocese of Viterbo. It was a devout and zealous parish priest, Benedict Baldi (1632-1694), a model of Counter Reformation priesthood, who conceived the idea of enriching his native town with a monastery of contemplative nuns. Through his efforts the ancient fortress of Vetralla was converted into a monastery. There he gathered eight young women to form a conservatory, until contemplative nuns could be found to instruct them in cloistered living. Three volunteers were eventually found in the Visitation of Turin, but when they arrived in Rome and were hospitably lodged by the Barberine, they availed themselves of woman's privilege to change their minds and settle in Rome. Instead the prioress of the Incarnation, Teresa of the Mother of God Rasponi, offered to provide assistance. Authorization was granted by Clement IX in February of 1699, and three Carmelites were dispatched to Vetralla: Minima of St. Mary Magdalen de' Pazzi (Anguillara), her sister Angela Catherine of Jesus and Angela Teresa of Jesus in Glory (Corsini). They returned to Rome in 1674 after the Vetralla community was well established and Sr. Mary Magdalen of the Blessed

Sacrament had been elected prioress. In 1695 the cornerstone was laid of a church, blessed in 1711. The benefactor of the monastery in this undertaking was Prince Livio Odescalchi, nephew of Innocent IX. The architect was Carlo Buratti, who also added a wing to the monastery completed around 1732.

The monastery of Mount Carmel in Vetralla was blessed to have for a while the spiritual ministration of the founder of the Passionists, St. Paul of the Cross (1694-1775).

Two important foundations in the South were Fasano and Capua.

Fasano in the diocese of Monopoli was originally a conservatory. Anna Maria Semeraro, the daughter of a shoemaker, dedicated herself to the interior life. For six years she was thought to be possessed by the devil. From Cherubino of the Cross, O.C.D., who had come to Fasano to preach during Lent she received the Discalced Carmelite habit and the name Cherubina of St. Joseph. When her example was followed, first by her three sisters, later by eight other women, Don Santi Mignozza, spiritual director of the group, conceived the idea of gathering them into a conservatory. Two sisters not only contributed their house, but themselves joined the community with the names Victoria of St. Peter and Baptista of the Passion (1681). After the number of sisters reached thirty, they moved to a new monastery provided by the municipality (1694). By the same token the community had outgrown the limits allowed by the constitutions of St. Teresa, and rather than reduce its numbers Cherubina adopted the constitutions of St. Mary's of Florence. After obtaining papal cloister on April 12, 1698, she died on the following July 15—ironically before she had finished her novitiate for solemn vows.

By that time however effective leadership of the community had been taken over by Rosemary of St. Anthony Serio (1674-1726). She was one of seven daughters of Anthony Serio, professor of medicine in Ostuni. Rosemary and another daughter he placed in the conservatory of Fasano (1690). During her novitiate Rosemary contracted the plague, that year rampant in the province of Bari, and was kept in solitary confinement to avoid contagion of the community. The solitude was entirely to her taste for prayer. Even at that age she was experiencing the mystical phenomena that were to play so large a role in her life. Sr. Cherubina enlisted a panel of theologians to examine the spirit of this ecstatic novice. They declared themselves satisfied. Nevertheless, Cherubina postponed Rosemary's oblation for four months. Even then Rosemary's troubles weren't over. Rumors of this visionary reached the vicar general, and when the priest he had sent to investigate the case submitted a negative report, he ordered Rosemary imprisoned, until definite measures could be taken. Eventually her sincerity and authentic virtue were vindicated. For seven years she suffered a sort of paralysis. Among her many mystical experiences she also received the stigmata. At the same time she performed many practical services to the community, acting in turn as portress, infirmarian, procurator, mistress of novices and finally at twenty-eight years of age, as prioress (1704), an office to which she was repeatedly elected until the end of her life. In her last illness she was visited by her aged physician father, whose skills however proved of no avail.

The cause of Rosemary's canonization, initiated in 1741, was not completed before the end of the century, when the activity of the Congregation of Rites came to a halt in the troubles of the times.

Rosemary's sister Magdalen who entered the conservatory with her was a year her senior and died at the age of thirty-five, also with a reputation for holiness (1673-1708). Her name in religion was Michela of St. Francis.

A younger sister Grace, born in 1687, entered the monastery of Fasano in 1704 and in 1730 founded a house in her native Ostuni. She wrote an account of the founding of Fasano and lives of some of its members illustrious for virtue. Her name in religion was Benedetta of the Holy Spirit.

Capua originated in 1734, when the ex-procurator general Salvatore Pagnani gathered a group of tertiaries into a conservatory under Mariangela of Divine Love as superior. He composed special constitutions, approved by Clement XIII in 1759 and published at Naples in 1761, which provided special penitential features such as going barefooted, practising extra fasts, etc. In 1763 the same pope raised the conservatory to the status of a cloistered monastery under the jurisdiction of the prior general.

The monastery, dedicated to the Archangel Gabriel, owed much to the generous patronage of Maria Amalia, Queen of Naples. When the court was in nearby Caserta, she would often join the community at meals and prayer. She assisted at the dedication of the church in 1752, when Peter Andrew Gauggi, Carmelite and distinguished theologian, preached the sermon. Her husband King Charles III of Spain took the monastery under royal protection and was wont to send from Spain, besides princely gifts, letters written in his own hand. His successor in the Kingdom of Naples, Ferdinand IV, and his consort Maria Carolina, continued the royal patronage.

Sister Mariangela made a second foundation at Grumo Nevano in the diocese of Aversa, also dedicated to the Archangel Gabriel. In 1764 she obtained permission from the Congregation of Bishops and Religious to visit it three times a year.

The glitteringly brilliant career of these two monasteries was of short duration. Both were swept away in the deluge that overtook royalty at the end of the century.

In the North an unusual development took place in the Republic of Venice, where no Carmelite nunneries had yet been founded. Responsible for this growth was Marietta Ferrazzi, known in religion as Angela Ventura of the Blessed Sacrament (1623-1688).

Luigi Ferrazzi, a weaver of Venice, and his wife, Magdalen Poli, produced no fewer than twenty-three offspring. Lest environmentalists become needlessly alarmed, let it be said at once that all, except Cecily and Marietta, perished in the disastrous plague of

1630. The two surviving orphans were placed, first with an uncle, later with a devout lady, Modesta Salandi, living near the Carmelite monastery. Her Carmelite spiritual director, Master Bonaventure Pinzoni, took a special interest in Marietta, struck by her intelligence and piety. She became proficient not only in all the feminine arts, so that she took over the management of Modesta's household, but under Master Pinzoni's tutelage learned reading, writing, and other scholarly attainments. Marietta was undoubtedly a young woman of strong character and unusual intelligence and piety. She was soon attracting other girls to her ideals of religious dedication and making practical plans for obtaining a house where they might live together. In 1643 at twenty years of age she signed a contract to purchase an abandoned Franciscan monastery for 3,000 ducats. Fifteen women joined Marietta in the conservatory dedicated to St. Teresa. They wore modest secular dress and recited the divine office according to the Carmelite rite, taught them by Master Bonaventure. The prudent virgin further guaranteed the stability of her house by placing it under the *ius patronato* of the Republic (1648). At the same time the restored church was declared fit for sacred functions. The sisters also adopted the habit of Carmel. Their original design was to follow the constitutions of St. Teresa, but eventually they accepted those composed by Filippini. In 1667 the monastery was declared cloistered and immediately subject to the general of the Order. Pinzoni was appointed commissary or delegate. The community had grown to thirty-seven, a new church had been built, the monastery enlarged. Before the death of the foundress the monastery included almost a hundred nuns. Among its chaplains or commissaries was Jerome Aimo, eminent Carmelite philosopher.

Besides this impressive achievement Sr. Mary Angela also has to her credit foundations at Verona (1654), Padua (1662), and Vicenza (1670).

For the nuns under its care the Mantuan Congregation published constitutions composed by John

Seraphina Bonastre, *d.* 1649,
foundress of the monastery of the Incarnation,
Valencia - Spain.

Mary of Jesus, 1589-1662,
of the monastery of the Mother of God, Piedrahita - Spain.
Engraving by R. Collin.

Baptist Guarguanti (Bergamo, 1656). The "Convertite" of Bologna also issued their own legislation (Bologna, 1738), as did the nuns of Sutri (Ronciglione, 1743).

The thirteen monasteries of the Congregation — Parma, Reggio Emilia, Brescia, Ferrara (San Gabriele), Mantua, Trino, Florence (San Barnaba), Sutri, Vinovo, Albino, Ferrara ("Convertite"), Ferrara (Santa Lucia), Bologna ("Convertite") — experienced a modest increment.

The monastery of St. Ursula in Bergamo had been founded in 1573. There thirty sisters followed a rule composed by St. Charles Borromeo. The Congregation undertook their direction in 1609. In 1656 they adopted the Carmelite habit and cloister. Two nuns, Michela Caria and Anne Felicity Marina, came from Albino to initiate them into the Carmelite way of life. The former became "abbess," the latter prioress. The monastery remained under the jurisdiction of the bishop.

In Camaiore the Congregation took over a pre-existing conservatory, founded in 1590 by Mary Magdalen Buonucelli. Leading spirit in the change which took place in 1634 was Jacinta Ricci, known in religion as Cherubina of the Lamb of God (1601-1663). Her childhood was passed in a climate of violence and instability. Her father Alderigo Ricchi was a native of Lucca, but moved to Sesto where he became governor of its abbey. When he was called away on affairs, he left Jacinta only recently born in the care of his brother Balduino. Six years later Alderigo died abroad—poisoned, it was rumored—followed shortly by his wealthy wife Justine. Balduino fell afoul of her brothers over his niece's inheritance, was obliged to flee to Portugal, and subsequently died a ruined man. Jacinta at twelve years of age ended up in the care of her two paternal aunts. When one of these died, the other placed her niece, aged fifteen, in the conservatory of Camaiore. The uncertainties of her childhood had only served to draw Jacinto closer to God, her only sure support. The *Spiritual Exercises* of St. Ignatius convinced her that she should embrace the religious life. She made her simple vows in 1634. Under the direction of Fr. John Baptist Cioni she made rapid progress in prayer, in time being favored even with mystical experiences. In 1628 she was made mistress of novices. She contracted the plague of 1631, which claimed 30,000 victims in the Republic of Lucca but spared her life. When the conservatory adopted the Carmelite rule and cloister, Sr. Cherubina was elected subprioress. Also due to her influence were a number of particular customs thenceforth observed in the monastery. The foundress, Sr. Mary Magdalen, lived under cloister for two years before her death in 1636, aged 62. From 1643, Cherubina served two terms as prioress. The last three years of her life were consumed by her last illness, caused it would seem by cancer of the breast. Her confessor, Fr. Jerome Fiorentini, assisted her in her last moments.

The monastery of Novellara was founded in 1668 at the request of Alphonse Gonzaga II, Count of Novellara and Bagnoli, and dedicated to his favorite saint, Teresa of Avila. Three tertiaries were fetched from Regio to make the foundation: Ursula Vecchi Mellari, Mary Magdalen Asassia and Angela Catherine Mellari, Ursula's daughter, who became respectively Ursula Mary of St. Joseph, Mary Magdalen of the Cross, and Angela Catherine of St. Joseph. They lodged in a house near the Carmelite church belonging to the confraternity of Our Lady of Mount Carmel. By 1674 six other women had joined the community. A monastery was begun in 1679; the Church of St. Teresa was blessed in 1684.

Ursula Vecchi was born in Reggio Emilia. After the death of her husband Anthony Mellari, she retired from the world, receiving the Carmelite tertiary habit in 1664. She lived only a year after entering the new monastery in Novellara. Mary Magdalen Adassia (1631-1695) had led a life of prayer and penance from her youth. She too became a Carmelite tertiary in 1664.

Holy Name monastery in Velletri was founded through the beneficence of Fulvio Mariola. On May 12, 1641, the first twelve nuns were given the Carmelite habit in a solemn ceremony in the cathedral. Among them was the widow of the founder, Lucile Assalonne, who took the name Anne in religion. A nun from the monastery of Sutri, Clara Androsilla, initiated the community into the Carmelite way of life.

On the other hand in 1616, Vinovo ceased to exist due to political conditions.

In 1661, the prior general, Jerome Ari, visited the monasteries of Brescia, Albino, Trino, Reggio and Florence. He would have liked to introduce the perfect common life, he told the 59 nuns in Brescia, but since the poverty of the community did not permit it, he contented himself with urging them to do so at the earliest possible opportunity. Meanwhile, they should make the *sproprio*, or declaration of their possessions, at least once a year. He was happy to find that the community of Albino (38 nuns) observed the perfect common life. "The state of the monastery," he noted about Trino with its community of 31, "although without the common life, otherwise did not require special decrees." The 73 nuns at Reggio Emilia, he decided, "needed rather to be encouraged in their life of virtue, since they are excellent religious, than to be corrected for defects." In the monastery of St. Barnabas in Florence with 69 nuns Ari considered it sufficient to make, in the words of his secretary Sebastian Fantoni Castrucci, "a pious and efficacious sermon."

About a dozen other monasteries appeared in other parts of Italy.

Little is known besides the name of the Retreat of the Presentation and the monastery of the Holy Family which existed at Asti (Piedmont) during the 18th century.

Pescia in the Republic of Lucca was founded in 1634 by the Carmelite Joseph Bonetti.

Pisa in the Archduchy of Tuscany, where the Carmelites had been present since 1249, finally received a monastery of nuns in 1630 through the initiative of John Baptist Petroni, later provincial of Tuscany. The foundation was affiliated to the

Order in 1633. Here Margaret Columba Lanfranchi (*d.* 1649) is remembered for holiness.

In the Papal States the bishop of Iesi, Peter Matthew Petrucci (d. 1701) in 1684 made Carmelite the Franciscan conservatory founded in 1660. The still existing monastery received papal cloister in 1697. There the famous Franciscan preacher St. Leonard of Port Maurice (1676-1751) erected one of his innumerable stations of the cross. Also in the diocese of Iesi, Montecarotto was founded in 1671 by the tertiary Frances of Jesus with the encouragement of the bishop, later Cardinal Alderano Cybo. Papal cloister was introduced in 1737. Orvieto was founded in 1662 by Sr. Teresa Magdalen of the Conception (*d.* 1683), formerly of a non-Carmelite conservatory.

In the Kingdom of the Two Sicilies the illustrious monastery of the Holy Cross of Lucca in Naples in 1637 made a second foundation in that city, the monastery of the Blessed Sacrament, which followed the reform of St. Mary della Vita. In 1627, Srs. Faustina Giscale and Felicity Bonelli, of the same monastery of the Holy Cross, had founded Somma. Castellamare, which already had a monastery, founded from the Holy Cross in 1560, in the 18th century seems also to have had a second monastery dedicated to St. Teresa.

Of interest is the relationship of St. Alphonsus Liguori to the two Neapolitan Carmels. For the monastery of the Holy Cross he composed a formula for the renewal of vows. A relative of his, Teresa Mary Liguori (1704-1724), belonged to the monastery of the Blessed Sacrament, "in which," in the words of the saint, "to the edification of all, regular observance was in a flourishing condition." In their youth their parents had given some thought to arranging a marriage between them. Many years later the saint wrote the biography of his cousin, so impressed was he by her virtue. In general outline his essay is like the other innumerable hagiographical works of the time, but is distinguished from them by its subdued tone and the prudent wisdom of its author. Evidently the monastery did not observe the common life, for Teresa's annuity had been placed in deposit for her, but she did not avail herself of it. At her request her spiritual director drew up a schedule of the day for her, which she faithfully observed in spite of aridity and darkness of spirit. She spent much time in prayer, "and as reward of the great love that she showed for prayer," writes the saint, "the Lord raised her to a high degree of contemplation."

Little is known of the Carmelite monasteries in Avellino (1623), Montecorvino (1766) and Solofra (1697).

In spite of its numerous friaries, Sicily for some reason never had many nunneries. To Messina and Palermo was added Siracusa, founded in 1717 as a conservatory by Sr. Carmela of the Blessed Trinity Montalto (*d.* 1780), assisted by Srs. Anna Maria and Felicity Gargallo. It received cloister in 1738 and followed the reform of Santa Maria della Scala, initiated by her friend Jerome Terzo.

At the beginning of our period the prior general, John Stephen Chizzola, during his visitation of Spain, 1594-1595, published a body of legislation for the nuns, *Decreta pro vita regulari sanctimonialium ordinis Carmelitarum amplificanda* (Seville, 1595).

The one hundred and seventy-eight decrees are divided into nine chapters, treating the divine office, community life, cloister, reception of novices, election of officers, education of girls, chaplains and confessors, administration of temporal goods, chapter of faults. A tenth chapter lists faults and their punishment. Ceremonies for clothing novices, making vows and imposing the veil end the volume. These constitutions, the first of their kind in Spain, undoubtedly filled a real need. To persons not versed in canon law they provided brief and practical guidelines to cloistered contemplative life, updated according to the council of Trent and developments within the Order itself.

Twice a day the nuns are to make a half hour meditation in choir and examine their consciences before retiring at night (ch. 1, nn. 14, 16). They are to confess once a month and to confessors of the Order only, except at the times of extraordinary confessions prescribed by the council of Trent (ch. 1, nn. 18-19). Frequent communion is recommended (ch. 1, n. 23). The nuns may support themselves by their labor; whatever individual nuns earn in this way is to be applied to their own needs first of all, then to the needs of the community (ch. 2, n. 3). This is obviously an adaptation of the custom of the deposit box of the friars. The giving of gifts by religious is prohibited, according to the decree of Pope Clement VIII (ch. 2, n. 8). The cloister is imposed on all the monasteries of women of the Order in Spain: "Monasteries of those nuns of our Order called *beatas* in Spain who neglect taking the veil, in order not to be obliged to cloister, to leave the monastery at will and to introduce extraneous persons into the cloister —such monasteries we will not permit for any reason.... We command the reverend provincials to oblige the said nuns to accept the veil as is customary in our Order and to observe the cloister.... If they refuse to comply, they are to be denied faculties to receive novices, so that they may die out and be reduced to nothing" (ch. 3, n. 45). Where the custom of educating girls in the monastery does not exist, it is not to be introduced, "for the more the nuns are free of these cares, the more they will be able to engage in the service of the Lord." Where such a custom exists, the conditions laid down by the Sacred Congregation are to be complied with (ch. 6). Chizzola himself arranged for a girl of eight to be educated in the monastery of St. Anne in Seville.

Spain added another dozen to its fourteen existing monasteries of cloistered nuns.

In the Castilian province a monastery of the old Carmel finally came into existence in Madrid, the nation's capital. A devout lady, Joan de Baraona, obtained permission from Pope Paul V to found a *beaterio*. In 1613 the provincial Anthony Pérez advised her with regard to the purchase of a house and provided the first six candidates from among his penitents, clothing them in the tertiary habit of Carmel. When Doña Baraona ill-advisedly admitted two married women separated from their husbands as members of the community, religious observance began to suffer due to the resulting distractions and lack of peace. The friars advised the sisters to move to another site (1617). It would seem that the foundress did not accompany them. In their new location the sisters acquired the chapel of St. Anthony the Abbot, where through a grill they recited the divine office according to the Carmelite rite. They followed the constitutions for nuns issued by Ferdinand Suárez (Seville, 1603), a translation from the Latin of John Stephen Chizzola's decrees of 1595. In 1627 the community passed under the jurisdiction of the ordinary as a step toward obtaining cloister. This consummation was achieved in 1630. On that occasion too new constitutions were composed (Madrid, 1630, reprinted 1757). In 1644 three Discalced nuns from the monastery of La Imagen in Alcalá de Henares took over the office of prioress, subprioress and mistress of novices, "in order to instruct them (the nuns) in the manner and form of recollection." It was at this time, it would seem, that the monastery adopted the Roman rite.

The history of the monastery of Madrid is closely bound up with its miraculous image of Our Lady of the Marigolds (*de las Maravillas*); in fact, the building was the gift of Philip IV in gratitude to this Virgin for recovery from illness (1646). The figure was about four and a half feet high. Mary supported the Child and held a flower in her hand. The nuns managed to safeguard their treasure during the vicissitudes of the 19th century, but in the civil war (1936-1939) the Reds discovered it in the patio of the monastery and burned it.

Some confusion exists about another monastery in Madrid, sometimes listed as Discalced. Popularly known as "Las Baronesas," the monastery owed its existence to the generosity of Baroness Beatrix de Sylveira, sister of the Carmelite scripture scholar. Fray Francisco Majuelo turned over to her royal patents which he had obtained for a monastery of Recollect Carmelite nuns and which she lacked for the monastery of forty nuns she was willing to provide. On August 15, 1651, six young noblewomen took possession of the premises and two days later received the Carmelite habit according to the mitigated rule. Four Discalced Trinitarian nuns filled the offices of authority until the neophytes learned the ways of contemplative life. The monastery, dedicated to the Nativity and St. Joseph, was placed under the jurisdiction of Archbishop Baltasar de Moscoso y Sandoval, who also wrote its constitutions (Madrid, 1662). Construction of a church and convent was undertaken by the architect John de Lobera in 1675, but took half a century to complete. The sisters lived the perfect common life. Well endowed, the monastery was intended for noblewomen of modest means, and no dowry was required.

In the third volume of his commentary on the Gospels (bk. 6, qu. 8) John de Sylveira pays his sister the compliment of applying to her the passage in Proverbs 31 about the "good wife," exemplifying every detail of scripture from her foundation in the calle Alcalá in Madrid.

After the death of St. Teresa (1582) the Incarnation of Avila was dominated by the personality of this great saint and dedicated to the perpetuation and imitation of her spirit and to the propagation of devotion to her. This direction was already indicated by the vicar general for Spain, Michael de Carranza, during a visit in 1588. On the occasion of the beatification of Teresa in 1614 the Carmelite friars and nuns vied with their Discalced brothers and sisters in the celebration of the event. No less a person than the learned Peter Cornejo de Pedrosa, professor at Salamanca, arrived to preach at the friary and the Incarnation. Paul de Aragón preached in the Discalced friary church. The canonization of the saint followed in 1622. When St. Teresa was declared patron of Spain, one of Carmel's most eloquent preachers, Christopher de Avendaño, delivered four sermons in Avila, one of them in the Incarnation.

Nevertheless relations between the friars and sisters at times were less than cordial. The chapter of 1624 discussed resigning the direction of the Incarnation as burdensome to the superiors of the province and moreover ineffective, because the nuns appealed from their decisions to other tribunals. In the end it was the nuns themselves who obtained from Pope Urban VIII a brief signed May 8, 1631, exempting them from the jurisdiction of the Order and placing them under that of the bishop. The prior of Avila, Diego Sánchez, protested and earned a rebuke from the definitory. The bishop, Francis Márquez de Gaceta, forbade the nuns under censure to have any communication with their Carmelite brothers. The thirteen nuns of the community of forty-three who wished to remain under the obedience of the Order were refused permission to transfer to another monastery.

Although Urban's brief adduces no reasons for the final break, it was apparently occasioned by an incident of a serious nature. In 1629 the prior of Avila, Celedón de los Santos, and a laybrother, Francis Ortiz, were found guilty of violating the cloister of the monastery by night and were condemned to the galleys. It was a dreadful scandal, for Celedón was a man of standing in the province, twice elected provincial. He lasted two years at his new occupation before being released to die.

New constitutions were published for the monastery (Salamanca, 1662).

The separation from the Order's jurisdiction of the Incarnation put an end to recurring family squabbles but also isolated it from the mainstream of the Carmelite tradition in which it had grown.

Among the many women of virtue and piety who graced the monastery of the Incarnation in Avila was Joan Baptist Jiménez (1577-1630). She was seven years old when her parents died and she was taken into the Incarnation by her sister Mary who was a servant there. Joan became the maid of Doña Agnes de Quesada, who reared her in a life of virtue and contributed to her dowry when she received the habit in 1604. This simple laysister was highly esteemed for holiness, her advice sought, her authority respected. Her funeral oration was delivered by Fray John García, lector of theology in the local Carmelite convent.

Piedrahita at this time produced a famous sister who however was sixty-two when she entered the monastery and already renowned as a visionary and holy person. Mary Muñoz was born of humble folk at Hoyos del Espino, a mountain village in the township of Piedrahita. Hoyos venerated Our Lady of the Hawthorn (*del Espino*), and Mary added this element to her surname. From childhood Mary was given to spiritual things and was gifted with rare mystical endowments. The Carmel of Piedrahita preserves a pall she made at the age of six with a painting of the Virgin, "as I saw her in heaven." The cattle she was set to watch used to wait patiently outside the church without straying, while she assisted at Mass and made her devotions. Poor as she was, she managed by dint of extra work to buy a silver lamp in Salamanca for the Virgin of the Hawthorn which was used in the church until 1735, when it was melted down to make a larger one. Mary was one of the witnesses who testified to miracles wrought in her favor by her beloved Virgin of the Hawthorn.

On two occasions her visions caused her to be imprisoned at Villatoro by the commissary of the Holy Office, John García, but she had friends in the episcopal city of Avila, among them the bishop himself, Francis Gammara (*d*. 1627), and his chapter. In the Incarnation there was Doña Teresa of the Holy Spirit de Oberón Tabera, whose extant letters testify to her esteem. Her regular confessor in Avila was the vicar general, John de Mendieta. When he was later transferred to the same office in Madrid, he introduced the humble mountain woman to Anne de Toledo, Marchioness of Villanueva del Río, who later entered the Discalced monastery at Alba de Tormes as Anna of the Cross.

In 1622, Mary went to live with her brother Joseph Muñoz (1593-1635), that year ordained a priest and assigned as pastor to Villatoro. Thereafter, she followed him on his assignments to Amavida (1626) and Bernui Zapardiel (1633). In the latter place Joseph died within the year of his arrival, venerated for his exemplary life. Mary returned to her native Hoyos del Espino, where she found still living the revered confessor of her childhood, Andrew Sánchez Tejado (1569-1635). It was he who ordered her to write—or rather, to dictate, for she could not write—the first account of her life, which she dedicated to the cathedral chapter of Avila. After Don Andrew's death Mary served the next curate Matthew de Contreras for twelve years.

Mary had already tried in vain to enter the Discalced monastery at Alba de Tormes. In 1651 she attempted again to become a religious, this time at Piedrahita. The provincial of Castile, Diego de Viña, gave his consent, but when she appeared on the scene, the vicar of the monastery, Francis de La Concha, would not accept this old unlettered woman, who moreover had no dowry. Doña Elizabeth Calderón, who favored her candidacy, took her into her cell as her maid. After he had heard Mary's confession, the vicar changed his mind as to her suitability for the religious life, and she was admitted as a laysister. Her profession as Mary of Jesus del Espino, May 5, 1652, turned out to be a splendid occasion on which her admirer, the mayor of Piedrahita, Diego Gómez, treated her and her family to a lavish banquet complete with musicians.

The nuns did not regret having admitted Sister Mary. She even managed to accumulate a dowry. At times they must have been amused at this simple peasant woman who stepped so unaffectedly over the threshold of the other world and who referred to the Lord as her "little Lamb." Through Doña Elizabeth's brother, Antonio Calderón, prior of the cathedral of Granada, Mary arranged to have the famous painter Alonso Cano reproduce her vision of Christ at the pillar of scourging, a painting still treasured by the nuns of Piedrahita. In 1675 at the behest of her superiors she dictated a second account of her life and spiritual itinerary. In the last four years of her life she became blind.

The general chapter of 1680 ordered Master Matthew Panduro y Villafañe to compile lives of Sister Mary of Jesus and of Sister Agnes and to send them to Master John Gómez Barrientos in Brussels, presumably to be printed there. Forty years elapsed before the appearance of Luis of

St. Teresa's (*d.* 1714) posthumous life of Mary of Jesus, based on materials gathered by Master Matthew Grogero (Salamanca, 1720).

The other nun referred to by the general chapter, Sister Agnes, of Fontiveros, never found her Boswell. She seems to have been the Agnes de Castellanos briefly mentioned by the Carmelite historian, John Baptist de Lezana.

The most remarkable development in the situation of the nuns in Spain was their growth in Catalonia, where they had been entirely lacking. These foundations are specifically stated in the sources to observe the perfect common life.

Founder of the monastery of Villafranca del Panadés was Master Martin Román, authorized to this end by the prior general, Theodore Straccio, on February 20, 1640. He would have looked to the province of Aragon for sisters to people his monastery, but Catalonia, overrun by the French, was cut off from the rest of Spain. Nothing daunted, he gathered six tertiaries into his monastery, blessed on April 22, 1643, and himself instructed them in the ways of Carmel according to the constitutions of St. Mary's in Florence. The first prioress was Mary Magdalen of St. Jerome. In 1647 the province accepted responsibility for these nuns, but in 1740 they passed under the jurisdiction of the bishop.

Master Román's makeshift community at Villafranca not only turned out to be excellent in itself but fruitful with life for others. Not long afterwards he called on it to provide the membership for a monastery he planned to found in Barcelona. For this purpose he obtained letters patent from the prior general, Leo Bonfigli, on August 19, 1645. The new monastery of the Incarnation was inaugurated on May 12, 1649, with two nuns from Villafranca, Gertrude of the Child Jesus (prioress) and Teresa of Jesus, and three novices, soon joined by five others. Master Román again undertook the direction of the sisters, living in a nearby house, and again introduced the Florentine constitutions. The plague of 1650 tried the infant community, claiming the life of Sr. Bendita of Christ who contracted the disease while caring for another sister. In 1674 a new chapel was inaugurated, the work of the master builder, John Termens. There Martin Román who had died in 1663 found his last resting place.

The prior of the reformed convent of Valls, Master Angelus Palau, whose sister Engracia of the Holy Spirit was a nun in Villafranca, in 1676 obtained a commission from the vicar general, Emile Giacomelli, to bring Carmelite sisters to Valls. One of his penitents, a wealthy widow of two marriages, Frances Saperas y Vidal, provided the financial means, to which Palau added an inheritance of his own. Doña Frances moreover and two cousins requested admission to the new foundation and with a candidate for the laysisterhood were sent to Barcelona to try their vocation. There on December 5, 1680, the four aspirants were given the habit, Doña Frances receiving the name Frances of the Presentation. Two days later, headed by the prospective prioress, Margaret of St. Elijah, they set out for Valls, passing through Villafranca, where they were joined by Engracia of the Holy Spirit and Anna Maria of Christ. The new monastery of the Presentation was inaugurated on December 15. Two years later the nuns from Barcelona and Villafranca returned to their original monasteries, and Sister Frances took over the reins. During her long term of office, 1682-1717, she placed the monastery on a firm foundation of fervent observance, becoming in effect its spiritual as well as its material foundress. In 1719 religious services were begun in the new chapel, to which the finishing touches were added only in 1781.

"That now makes three monasteries of reformed Carmelite nuns that Your Reverence has in this your province," the provincial, John de Cáncer, wrote to the prior general, Ferdinand Tartaglia, January 4, 1681. "They shed much luster and esteem on our holy habit for the great virtue and perfection with which they live, observing with all rigor the common life." On July 24, 1683, Cáncer was able to report to Tartaglia the foundation of another reformed monastery earlier that month in Vich.

Master Martin Román's first efforts at founding

a cloistered monastery of the Order had been made in Vich. He had already obtained permission from the city council (1628) and had found a benefactress, Doña Maria Osona, widow of Dr. Francis Bergada, when the nuns he wished to import from Aragon refused to renounce the jurisdiction of the Order in favor of that of the bishop. Discalced nuns who had no such reservations fell heir to the fruits of his efforts (1637). In spite of the fact that the city thus already had a Carmelite monastery, municipal authorities in 1663 authorized putting into effect a legacy left in 1660 by Francis Llucía de Codina y de Pons, canon of the cathedral of Vich, benefactor also of the Incarnation of Barcelona. The Discalced Joseph of the Conception (d. 1689) was the architect of the monastery which however suffered many delays in its construction. Conventual life was finally initiated on July 1, 1693, by Sister Mary of the Cross, of Villafranca, and by four professed nuns and three novices of Barcelona. The benefactor, Canon Codina, fortunate heir to the sisters' prayers and sacrifices, was entombed in the chapel constructed between 1731 and 1741. The retable of the main altar picturing the Presentation, title of the foundation, was the work of Mariano Colomer.

Among the dedicated women who peopled the Catalonian monasteries Eulalia of the Cross (1669-1725) is especially remembered and revered. Her parents, John Mora and Magdalen Xammar, united two noble families of Corbera and Gerona respectively. In their case the old hagiographer's chestnut that they were as noble for virtue as for blood is no cliché, at least if the fruit of their union is any indication. Of their ten children, all girls, three became Cistercians, three Hieronymites and three Carmelites. Of two boys by John's previous marriage Francis become a Jesuit and eloquent orator. Clementia, Ignatia and Eulalia entered the Incarnation of Barcelona. As a child of nine Clementia accompanied the foundresses to Vich, was professed as Clementia of Jesus and Mary (1689) and in time became prioress. Eulalia was seven when she entered the Incarnation and was professed in 1685 at the canonical age of sixteen. She became a religious of outstanding virtue and exalted prayer. Her writings in two volumes are preserved in a copy made by her spiritual director Joseph Cabrer (d. 1769). Eulalia was prioress in 1714 when the community was forced to evacuate the monastery during the bombardment of the city by the troops of Philip V.

At the beginning of the 17th century the province of Aragon counted three cloistered monasteries: the Incarnation and St. Anne's in Valencia and Onteniente.

Foundress of the monastery of St. Michael in Sariñena in 1612 was Sr. Frances Pérez de Botanos who subsequently became the first prioress of the monastery of the Incarnation and St. Michael in Huesca. This foundation was made in 1622 by the local prior, Peter Jerome Sobrino, with moneys donated by Doña Anne de Santa-pau, who herself received the habit there. In 1623 the Confraternity of St. Michael turned over its church to the nuns. In 1656 a second Carmelite monastery, dedicated to the Assumption, rose in Huesca, when eleven nuns under Sr. Beatrix Pastor opted to live under episcopal jurisdiction.

With the foundation of the Incarnation of Zaragoza the province acquired a monastery in this important center, the equivalent of Valencia. Doña Anne de Carrillo, widow of Peter García and penitent of Fray Anthony Oliván y Maldonado, desired to donate her house for a monastery which she herself could afterwards enter. Her brother, Don Martin de Carrillo, canon of the cathedral, whom she consulted, at first attempted to dissuade her on the grounds that she was too old (fifty-seven) to adjust to religious life, and that her house was too small to accommodate a large community. Later he reconsidered, and on July 11, 1615 the new monastery opened with nuns fetched from the Incarnation of Valencia: Seraphina Andrea Bonastre, prioress; Agnes de Ariño, subprioress and novice mistress; Catherine de Horto, bursaress; Magdalen Sanz, portress. Besides Doña Anne and two nieces, three other young women entered the cloister that day. The monastery of the Incarnation of Zaragoza in time came to number about one hundred nuns and ran into serious financial difficulties, requiring constant financial assistance from the province.

"He would do a distinctive service," Fr. Hoppenbrouwers writes of this monastery, "who would dedicate a monograph to this Carmelite community and its more important members, among them the three Escobar sisters," Mary, Margaret and Marianne. Their mother, Marianne Villalba y Vincente (1565-1623), was herself a person of no mediocre piety. Not only did three of her children become Carmelite nuns, but her second husband Caspar Escobar (*d.* 1620) was led by her to take a serious interest in the Christian commitment. Doña Marianne was a tertiary of the Order of Minims, and her spiritual director was John Pérez of the same Order. The link between Carmel and her daughters seems to have been Fray Anthony Oliván who knew Caspar Escobar and often spoke to him in enthusiastic terms of the religious fervor of the newly founded monastery of Carmelite nuns.

Of the three sisters the eldest, Mary (1599-1654), entered the Incarnation at the relatively mature age of seventeen and was professed the following year, 1618. Of a serene character, instinctively inclined to contemplation, Mary was a pillar of strength to her younger sister. Her account of her interior trials and graces of prayer has been published. Marianne (1603-1660) was professed the year after Mary, but had been living in the monastery from the age of fourteen. She long survived her short-lived sisters. At the age of nine Margaret (1608-1641) was admitted to Holy Communion by the famous Carmelite preacher, Christopher de Avendaño, in Zaragoza to preach for the Confraternity of the Blessed Sacrament in the parish of St. Paul, to which the Escobars belonged. The next year, as an *educanda*, she followed her older sister into Carmel and was given the habit in 1620. Margaret's vocation was not an easy one. Even after profession in 1624, she had several relapses before she committed her-

Rosa Maria Serio, 1674-1726,
of the monastery of St. Joseph, Fasano - Italy.
Engraving by Nicholas Billy
from a painting by John Sorbi.

The Carmelite nun is distinguished for her devotion
to Our Lady. Carmel of St. Anne,
Carpineto Romano - Italy.

self whole-heartedly to the contemplative vocation. She was helped over the first hurdles by a skilled spiritual director, Dominic Avertanus Lansana, who later joined the reform. Afterwards entrusted with the delicate task of guiding these sisters, all gifted with mystical graces, was Bartholomew Viota (*d.* 1641). To his suggestion we owe their accounts of their interior life.

Three cousins of the Escobar sisters, daughters of their sister Emerantia, also entered the Incarnation: Marianne (*d.* 1659), Margaret (*d.* 1664) and Gertrude (*d.* 1693) Beltrán.

Seraphina Bonastre, first prioress of Zaragoza, was born in Valencia, the youngest of three daughters of Peter Bonastre and Magdalen Sistero. Her first guides in the spiritual life were an aunt and Jerome de Mur, S.J. Feeling called to the religious life, she entered the Incarnation of Valencia and in 1588 made her profession in the hands of Michael Carranza, the provincial. Spiritual directors in these first years of her religious life were John Sanz and, in his absence, Angelus Palacios. Such was her progress in religious perfection that she was chosen to head the sisters selected to make the foundation in Zaragoza. She established the new community in great fervor of spirit, herself providing the lead in all things. She indicated her readiness to comply with the request of Doña Anna de Carrillo that the monastery be modelled on the usages of the Discalced, "since in truth we are all shoots springing from the same tree, the roots and foundation of which is the continual meditation on the most holy life of Christ Our Lord. It is to this that we are principally obliged by the rule under which we all strive and which in this matter has not been mitigated for the Observants." Seraphina's autobiography and story of her soul, edited by Peter de Oxea, S.J., and preceded by a brief account of her life by Joseph Andrés, S.J., was published by Raymund Lumbier (Zaragoza, 1675).

Sister Mary Joseph of Jesus (*d.* 1625), to adduce a final example of holy members of the Zaragoza community, was born Mary Navarro in Sabiñán

(Calatayud). She seems to have been early orphaned, for it was her relatives that placed her in service to Doña Anne de Funes, wife of Don John Muñoz, whose domicile was Zaragoza. Doña Anne treated Mary with every consideration and allowed her full freedom to lead the life of prayer and penance to which she was inclined. Two servants whose misdeeds she had discovered in what seemed an unaccountable way delated her as a witch to the Inquisition, but upon examination by Licentiate Michael de San Pedro she was cleared of any diabolical association. At an unknown date Mary Navarro married, as her biographer Joseph Andrés discovered to his embarassment, after he had published her life celebrating her unsullied virginity. The death of her husband in 1614 was probably the signal for her entrance as a laysister into the Carmelite monastery in Zaragoza (1618 or 1619). Little is known of her external existence; her ample biography is exclusively concerned with her interior life. Even the usual chapters on the practice of the virtues which yield particulars on the subject's relations with others are wanting. The devil plays a large role in her life, or is considered to do so. Sister Mary Joseph's spiritual director was Master Michael Pérez de Artieda. His account of her supernatural experiences, on which Andrés bases his book, includes letters to him and to others by his penitent. Master Nicholas Ricarte, ordinary confessor of the monastery, assisted her in her last agony, April 18, 1625.

Francis Pastor of the province of Aragon published constitutions for Carmelite nuns based on those of Ferdinand Suárez (see below) and the decrees of Chizzola (Valencia, 1731).

In 1600, Andalusia had more Carmelite monasteries than all the other Spanish provinces put together. By the end of the century this could no longer be said, though it still had the most monasteries of any single province in spite of only a modest growth. Three nunneries were added to those already existing in Ecija, Granada, Seville

(Incarnation), Antequera, Aracena, Osuna, Utrera, Seville (St. Anne's).

The provincial Ferdinand Suarez published *Constitutions of the Carmelite Nuns of the Regular Observance, Composed by Apostolic Authority* (Seville, 1603) which made available in Spanish Chizzola's decrees of 1595. At the general chapter of 1609 the cardinal protector Dominic Pinelli had some reservations about the apostolic authority attributed to the constitutions.

The Incarnation of Granada published its own *Perpetual Constitutions* (Granada, 1735).

In 1773 Osuna undertook to observe the common life.

Villalba de Alcor was founded from St. Anne's, Seville, in 1619. There Sr. Beatrix Tinoco (1577-1622) had long desired to live in a monastery where the perfect common life was observed. When she learned from her sister Agnes that their uncle García Jiménez Franco planned to subsidize the founding of a monastery in Villalba del Alcor near her native Mancanilla, she convinced him that it should be Carmelite. The contract agreed to by the provincial Diego de Miranda stipulated that Beatrix should be prioress for life and that the special statutes she had drawn up for perfect observance be enforced together with the constitutions of the Order. Three professed nuns, one novice and two postulants accompanied Sr. Beatrix from Seville to form the new community.

From Villalba a foundation was made in 1662 at Cañete la Real through the generosity of Melchor de Rojas y Saavedra, former rector of the University of Osuna and native of Cañete, who contributed buildings which had been a tavern. The provincial Estacio Guitérrez summoned four nuns from Villalba under Sr. Catherine of Jesus. Another, Jerónima Román, who aspired to live the reformed life, came from Antequera and took the name Jerónima of St. Elisha. The new reformed monastery was dedicated to the Blessed Sacrament.

Sr. Catherine of Jesus (1598-1676) was born in Seville of the noble Viscayan family of the Zabaletos. After the death of her parents she was reared by an aunt, a devout woman who brought her niece with her into a *beaterio*. A Dominican confessor encouraged Catherine's desire to enter a cloistered monastery. She would no longer have been a child but a mature person when she entered the monastery of Villalba, which however, probably had not been long founded, for the common and recollected life had still not been firmly established. Catherine labored so efficaciously to bring this about that the provincial was able to apply there confidently for the foundresses of a reformed monastery in Cañete. This monastery too Catherine, several times elected prioress and novice mistress, confirmed in the same tradition of reform.

Among the members of this community excelling in virtue was Sr. Josepha Jerónima of St. Florence (1640-1725), born in Marchena of noble parents, Louis de Escobar and Elvira de Vega. She was seven when a plague left her and a younger sister orphans in the care of an uncle. Eventually Josepha was taken in by a noble couple of Cañete La Real, John de Argote and Mary de Rojas. The spiritual director of the latter, Francis de Rojas, was impressed by the precocious piety of the child and undertook to lead her along the way of prayer. Josepha was twenty-two years old when she arranged to enter the monastery the Carmelites were planning to open in Cañeta. Being on the spot, she was installed in the building before the sisters arrived. She used to say, "Before the mother foundresses appeared, I had already gathered half a *cahiz* of grain." She entered the Order as a laysister, a rare decision for a noblewoman to take. Her life of humble labor was undistinguished for external achievements but rich in spiritual gifts bestowed by the Spirit in the solitude she loved. A diary of her interior life was kept by Fray Louis de Avendaño, first vicar of the monastery.

In spite of the fact that the Order counted many friaries in the New World, the sisters had never set foot there. The Carmelites of Spain had not been allowed to make permanent foundations in the colonies, and Portugal which might have provided sisters for Brazil had few monasteries. There was also the practical difficulty of supporting cloistered monasteries in a society still struggling to establish itself.

The foundation of a cloistered Carmelite monastery in America came about somewhat after the manner of Las Baronesas in Madrid, which however it preceded. In 1642 the noble lady Anna de Lanzós donated her palace for a monastery in San Juan de Puerto Rico. Royal permission was obtained in 1646. When efforts to import Carmelite nuns from Seville proved unavailing, three Dominicans, Louise de Valdelomar, Mary de Ayala and Jerónima de Otañes, were fetched from Queen of Angels monastery in Santo Domingo to initiate religious life according to the Carmelite rule (1651). Doña Anna entered the monastery as Anna of Jesus, together with her sister Antonia of the Incarnation. After the Dominicans returned to their monastery, Anna of Jesus took over as prioress. The monastery, dedicated to St. Joseph, does not seem to have had cloister. The Dominicans laid a firm foundation of Carmelite life, for the monastery of St. Joseph, isolated, unaided, flourished as none other until the present day.

A fourth monastery, Guimarāes, was added to Beja, Lagos and Tentúgal to complete the growth of the Order's nunneries in Portugal.

In 1685 a conservatory for needy girls was founded in Guimarāes under the patronage of Francis Antuñes Torres. Two years later the inmates received the Carmelite tertiary habit. In time a church was built and cloisters added, so that in 1704 the conservatory became a cloistered monastery. The nuns made solemn profession in the name of the Carmelite vicar general for Portugal, Master Anthony of the Incarnation. When the archbishop of Braga understandably challenged this informal arrangement, Benedict XIII sanated the situation, August 3, 1726. In 1745 the monastery passed under the jurisdiction of the bishop.

The Portuguese nunneries seem to have been affected even less than the friaries by the winds of reform abroad in other parts of the Order. In Béja, which was probably only a mirror of religious life as found in the other nunneries, the common life was not observed. Noble and wealthy nuns still had their own "houses" or living quarters where they lived with their maids and infant candidates to religious life, often their nieces. Yet this monastery produced two of the most famous Carmelite nuns of the century.

Marianne of the Purification Azevedo (1623-1695) was born in Lisbon, the daughter of a wealthy goldsmith. The eldest of eleven children of Antonio Azevedo by his second wife, Maria da Cruz, Marianne remained at home until she was forty years old, living a life of retirement and prayer. For a while (1661) she wore the Theatine habit, until Rome forbade the practice. When her brother Francis Azevedo, who was a Carmelite, became chaplain of the monastery of Our Lady of Hope (*Esperança*) in Beja, he persuaded her to enter it. She was professed on November 29, 1664, a mature woman with long experience of prayer and penance. In Carmel, Marianne did not find the opportunity for the prayer and solitude she longed for. The *Esperança* was a sprawling complex of "houses," or living quarters, containing over a hundred nuns. Together with another young nun she was designated to share the house of Sister Brites da Graça and her maid. The continual visits and gossip sessions were a distraction to Marianne who longed only to be alone with her Divine Spouse. Her efforts to be moved to the common dormitory, her ecstasies which set her off from the others, did not endear her to her companions, and she was forced to endure much petty persecution.

In Frei Anthony de Escobar (1618-1681), named confessor of the Esperança in 1667, she found a sympathetic friend, who unfortunately proved to be her worst enemy. Instead of making little of her visions, ecstacies and locutions, he encouraged them, even publicized them, putting them to the test in public. Inevitably the Inquisition turned its attention to this visionary nun who was causing such an uproar. The investigation, initiated in October, 1668, ended with a whimper. Its final stage began in February of 1670, when the Inquisitor John da Costa Pimenta appeared at the monastery door to question Marianne and its inmates. He found that the culprit herself had been made mistress of novices. Contrary to previous evidence, the sisters had nothing but praise for Marianne. Close investigation into an alleged fast by Marianne showed that in fact she had had absolutely nothing to eat the whole of the previous November. The dry well of the monastery, too, proved to contain water as a result of her prayers. After seven weeks of questioning, of which no written record remains, the Inquisitor with a word of assurance to the nuns returned to Evora, and nothing further was heard of the matter. Her contemporaries took this as a victory for Marianne. Recently it has been conjectured that Pimenta, experienced in the matter of visions, genuine or otherwise, concluded that Marianne was deluded but sincere and virtuous (the two conditions are not necessarily mutually exclusive) and persuaded the *mesa* of the Inquisition of Evora to bury the process in the archive. "In our case," Mauricio Bruni concludes, "the tribunal of the Holy Office is in no way the horrible monster it is usually pictured to be."

Marianne continued her life as before without interference from the Inquisition, and her reputation for sanctity grew with the years. After two terms as novice mistress she served as prioress from 1680 to 1683. Marianne was by nature gentle and affable, in spite of her implacable asceticism, but she proved an effective leader who brought greater calm and recollection to the monastery. Her most distinctive achievement was the establishment of a "desert," or area within the monastery precinct with cells to which the sisters could retire at will for solitude, prayer and penance. There Marianne spent the last twelve years of her life, finally in possession of the precious pearl of contemplation for which she had exchanged her all. There too she was visited in 1695 by the prior general, John Feijóo de Villalobos, who spent a long time in conversation with her and on leaving assured the sisters that he had been rewarded for all the fatigues of the visitation. The decrees of the subesquent provincial chapter under his presidency, treating at length the spiritual care of the nuns, may perhaps be traced to this conversation.

Marianne left a spiritual diary begun in 1668 at the insistence of Escobar and ending with the year 1675. In her last years her mystical seizures seem to have decreased. Frei John da Luz had inherited the difficult task of directing this extraordinary woman.

The influence of Marianne in the *Esperança* lived on in such persons as her friend, Louise of St. Ignatius Pereira Serrão (*d.* 1691), and her disciples, Catherine Mary of St. Joseph Luiz (*d.* 1708) and Marianne of the Blessed Sacrament Touro Nogueira (*d.* 1708). Like Marianne, Mary of St. Joseph Cabo Sebolinho Bayoa (*d.* 1683) observed perfect poverty, and Joan Joseph of the Conception Gomes Baysa (*d.* 1719) lived as an anchoress.

It is not certain how long Marianne's desert continued to exist. Perpetua da Luz may be alluding to it when she expresses her disapproval of reforms which not all can observe and which consequently cause division. This woman, whose harrowing spiritual itinerary had led her through the valley of the shadow of death, held a serene and balanced view with regard to the minutiae of renewal, urging the reform of self and the observance of the common life which united all in charity.

Perpetua da Luz was a native of Beja itself. Her parents, Manuel da Costa Diniz and Leonor de Jesus, were Carmelite tertiaries and reared their daughter in religious ways. It was only after the death of her father to whom she was greatly devoted that Perpetua at the relatively mature age of twenty entered the *Esperança*. With the reception of the habit on October 22, 1704, she began a comfortable and undistinguished religious life, until August 23, 1719, when she heard a sermon which proved a turning point in her life. She exchanged her elegant habit for one of rough wool, emptied her cell of its luxuries and by a public act of renunciation surrendered her possessions to the monastery. Two nuns were assigned by the prioress, Ursula Teresa of St. Anthony, to see to her wants, since there was no provision for the common life. She also undertook a regime of fierce penitential practices which ruined her health and probably occasioned a seven year period (1722-1729) of hallucination ascribed to the devil. During its final and worst phase, beginning April 27, 1727, she performed actions totally out of character and was convinced that she was possessed. Like many another holy but over zealous person she came to the belated conclusion that "great penances are only great illusions."

Meanwhile, however, she had experienced her first ecstasy in 1721, which initiated a series of supernatural phenomena ending only with her death. Her account of her spiritual experiences, written at the command of her spiritual directors, John de Souza and Joseph de Aguiar, perished in the earthquake of 1755, not however until part of it had been included in her biography by Joseph Pereira. "The writings of the Carmelite nun," writes Fr. Pablo Garrido, O.Carm., "despite their tormented psychology, strike one by their perfect orthodoxy, lived during difficult times. Unconsciously she contributed to dissipating the fog of Quietism and specifically the doctrine of pure love. She makes a plea for loving God because he is He Who Is, but also for loving the virtues, because they are the work of God."

Beyond the Italian and Iberian peninsulas Carmelite nunneries remained few and far between. The marvelous renascence of Carmelite life there, that expressed itself, among other ways, in the multiplication of friaries, had little similar resonance in terms of monasteries of nuns. The presence of the feminine branch of Carmel remained restricted mainly to the provinces in which John Soreth had erected the first cloistered monasteries: Belgium, Francia, and Touraine. The spread of Carmelite nunneries in France was hardly favored by the monopoly the influential Discalced nuns claimed to have for making Carmelite foundations outside Brittany.

At the beginning of the 17th century the province of Francia counted monasteries at Liège and

Huy. The latter became the seed bed of a luxuriant growth. From Huy Dinant was founded in 1605. It was only poetic justice. Dinant had been established in 1455, but when it was sacked and burned by the troops of Charles Count of Charolais in 1466, part of the community took refuge in Huy. Other foundations from Huy were Rochefort (1626), Ciney (1630) and Fumay (1633). Ciney became Discalced in 1649. All these houses lay in the Belgian diocese of Namur, with the exception of Fumay in the diocese of Reims. In 1683 the common life was introduced in Huy.

In Reims too was situated Charleville, founded in 1620 through the munificence of Charles I Gonzaga, Duke of Mantua.

In the territory of the province of Touraine lay the monasteries of Nantes and Vannes, venerable foundations of Bl. Frances d'Amboise, who had been at pains to secure the right for her sisters to choose their confessors from any province. Such confessors were thereby absolved from obedience to their provincials. The privilege had made sense in previous centuries, but became an anachronism and a source of endless controversy, after the French provinces were reformed.

As provincial, Philip Thibault was himself responsible for the foundation in 1622 of the monastery of the Holy Sepulchre at Rennes. It had the benefit of the spiritual ministrations of the exemplary members of the nearby friary, cradle of the reform of the Order. Not the least solicitous was Brother John of St. Samson, whom Thibault often led to the monastery. Two of John's spiritual daughters, foundresses who had come from Vannes, were Valence of St. Clare (1601-1628) and Gilette of St. Francis (1600-1647). Under the direction of Brother John, Valence made great progress in the interior life. Such was her love of God that she could not hear it spoken of without falling into ecstasy. One of these occasions was witnessed by Dominic of St. Albert. She filled a number of offices in the community and in spite of her youth became prioress.

Even before she had entered the monastery of Nazareth at Vannes 1617, Gilette had dedicated herself to a life of prayer and penance. At Rennes she too came under the influence of Brother John and other early figures in the Observance of Rennes. "The axis of her spiritual life was Christ," writes Fr. Vital Wilderink. "It was her union to Christ that determined her relation to the eternal Father and the Virgin Mary. The Holy Spirit was her friend, her intimate. She felt herself raised by the Word and the Holy Spirit before the majesty of God the Father and presented to him for adoption as his child in a special manner." Her mystical union with God did not lessen her concern for her fellow man. She wrote a *Treatise* on the State and Union of the Church which brought upon her the disapproval of her superiors and sisters. This tract and other spiritual writings have apparently been lost.

It may have been either to Valence or to Gilette that John of St. Samson wrote "one of his most beautiful letters of direction," to quote John's biographer, Suzanne Bouchereaux.

In 1627, Thibault become vicar of Nazareth in Vannes. That same year he arranged for the monastery to make a second foundation at Ploërmel under the title of Bethlehem. It became Thibault's favorite monastery, "his beloved Bethlehem," to which he often returned.

Leader of the little band of four foundresses was Joan of the Assumption (*d.* 1645). She was greatly devoted to the Passion and while meditating on this mystery experienced in her body the sufferings of Christ. She is also remembered for her serene and imperturbable spirit. When a violent storm (believed to be raised by evil spirits) shattered the windows and overturned the bells of the Carmelite church in Loudun and caused much damage in Ploërmel, Joan remained unmoved amid the general panic.

Biographical sketches of a few of the sisters in this fervent community have come down to us. When the sisters enroute to found their monastery in Ploërmel stayed in the house of her father, Joan of the Child Jesus (*d.* 1670) was so impressed by their conversation and conduct that she followed in their footsteps.

On her way to arrange the contract of her

betrothal to the nobleman John Hallon de Lestria-gat, Marie Therese of St. Stephen (d. 1673) stopped in at the monastery of Ploërmel to visit relatives of her financé. In the parlor she seemed to hear an interior voice saying, "You will die in this monastery." "It will have to be quick," she reflected wryly, "because I'm leaving in a moment." Later a messenger met her underway with the news that John was gravely ill. She arrived in Rennes in time to have him die in her arms. After this she decided to enter the monastery of Ploërmel. She was guided in this decision by Stephen of St. Francis Xavier who had assisted her lover in his last hours.

Perrine of St. Teresa (d. 1673), of noble family, was devoted to the poor. At times her generosity was such that it was to be feared that the sisters would go hungry, but the larder (miraculously, the sisters said) always contained enough for the needs of all. Marie of the Child Jesus (d. 1683) served as novice mistress and prioress. In keeping with her name she was especially devoted to the Infant Jesus, a devotion the Touraine friars imported into the monasteries under their care, and had a confraternity erected in the church. Calliope of St. Francis (d. 1706) was so attracted to solitude that she made a vow not to leave her cell except for community acts and the claims of charity. This did not hinder her from being elected novice mistress and prioress.

For the nuns of Rennes and Ploërmel Stephen of St. Francis Xavier composed his *Exhortations monastiques* (Rennes, 1687).

In 1600 the sisters of Vannes elected John de Launay, ex-provincial, their confessor. He became their vicar in 1607 and served in that capacity until his death twenty years later. Launay did much to raise the spiritual level of the monastery, introducing many of the principles and practices of the Observance of Rennes. This process was continued and perfected by Thibault. In true style of the Touraine reform he set about providing structures apt for religious life. Nazareth was poorly arranged and unhealthy. Two or three sisters shared the same small cell. Thibault erected adequate buildings and separated the novitiate from the quarters of the professed. Needless to say he stressed the interior life and the practice of prayer. He recommended the *Spiritual Combat* and commented it often. Unfortunately these conferences seem to have been lost. On his death in 1638, Thibault was interred under the main altar of the monastery church.

The monasteries in the province of Touraine, contemporary to the spiritual renewal of France and beneficiaries of the ministrations of their brothers in the initial fervor of reform, were unequalled in the quality of their religious life.

In the territory of the Flandro-Belgian province venerable nunneries existed in Bruges, Gelderen and Vilvoorde. When the Wallo-Belgian Vicariate was erected in 1681, Namur fell within its ambit.

Margaret of the Mother of God, of Sion monastery in Bruges, died in 1647, only twenty-eight years old, but the memory of her holy life remained green. Joan of the Cross gave Margaret her spiritual formation. She was long prioress and died with a reputation for holiness in 1653. The catalog of the Sion library, dated 1723, has survived and may provide an indication of the spirituality of the monastery.

It was from Bruges that the noted Carmelite historian, Daniel of the Virgin of the Virgin Mary, in 1663 obtained sisters for a foundation in Louvain.

During the wars between the Spanish Netherlands and Holland and France, Vilvoorde often lay in the path of contending armies. The Carmelite sisters were forced to flee to Brussels, Antwerp, and Mechelen in 1621, 1635, 1667, 1695, 1702. In spite of these peregrinations they managed to build a new church, consecrated in 1671. During the 18th century the sisters enjoyed a well-earned peace and twice—in 1728 and 1778—celebrated anniversaries of their miraculous statue of Our Lady of Consolation, acquired (it was thought) in 1228.

Two sisters of Vilvoorde whose fame for sanctity lived after them were Mary of St. Joseph (*d.* 1660), of noble parentage, who became prioress, and Petronella van der Elst (*d.* 1674), a laysister whose brother Josse was abbot of Grinberg in Brabant.

Vilvoorde provided the sisters for a new foundation in Boxmeer. In 1666 the pastor of that town, Anthony Peelen, noted for zeal and charity, had bequeathed his property "Elzendaal" for a monastery of nuns, and the provincial, Francis of Bonne Espérance, had no difficulty in obtaining it for the Order from Countess Magdalen van den Bergh, who admitted to "a particular inclination and affection for the sisters of the Order of Mount Carmel" (1671). On September 1, 1672, Michael of St. Augustine, named vicar by Francis, appointed four sisters under Petronilla of St. Joseph for the proposed foundation. The roads between Vilvoorde and Boxmeer were beset with roving bands of marauding soldiers, but from her anchorhold in Mechelen Maria Petyt, Carmelite tertiary and mystic, assured the sisters that they would arrive safely, as indeed happened on September 9. In that Catholic island of the Protestant North the sisters undertook the education of girls. Cloister was imposed in 1678. In 1682 the cornerstone of a new monastery and chapel was blessed. Several times in the course of the 18th century Boxmeer provided asylum for the community of Gelderen, fleeing before the disturbances of war.

A sister of the monastery of Namur noted for holiness was Sr. Anne Loison (1552-1631). From Namur Marche was founded in 1620. Of the nuns of this monastery Celestine of St. Simon Stock composed a biography (1678) of Scholastica of St. Elijah (1613-1650) in which he also provided a brief sketch of the life of Catherine of St. Paul. Our Lady of Mercy in the monastery of Marche was credited with many supernatural favors, which after examination by doctors and theologians were approved by Bishop Ferdinand of Liège.

In Germany the Stricter Observance produced no monastery of nuns, and the house in Cologne of tertiary sisters with simple vows remained the only Carmelite establishment for women in Germany. During his visit there in 1603 Sylvio found that the seven sisters wore no veil, had no cloister, and went out with permission of the prioress. He ordered the Little Office of Our Lady recited in Latin rather than in German. In 1653, Filippini authorized the sisters to adopt the habit of the Touraine nuns and to wear the black veil, hence from that point onward they were probably cloistered contemplative nuns.

On the other hand the Polish Carmelites introduced their sisters to their native country. As early as 1632 the newly elected provincial, Bartholomew Galankowic, requested authorization of the prior general to found a monastery in Lwów, in which he proposed to enclose a group of noble young ladies, tertiaries of the Order. Straccio actually accorded the permission to Nicholas Dabrowski three years later, but the project does not seem to have been realized until 1677. A Carmelite monastery was established in Dubno in 1702 through the munificence of Theophila Ludovica, Countess of Ostrog and Zastaw.

Chapter VI

THE WAR ON THE NUNS

By the end of the 17th century the fervor of the Catholic Reformation had spent itself, and the 18th century ushered in the Age of Enlightenment. Weakened Christianity was no match for the fashionable Deism, rationalism, and Freemasonry, which reasoned against and railed against a supernatural, revealed religion. Society was still religious, but 18th century absolute monarchs, deeply imbued with Illuminism and often only vaguely Christian, followed the lead of Emperor Joseph II, "the sacristan," and sought the nationalization of the Church and its complete subjection to the State. Religion was seen only as useful for maintaining law and order in society. This theory still lay behind the policies of Napoleon, but 19th century liberalism, having no such lingering remnants of faith, without more ado banished the Church entirely from public life and created the secular State. The Church was no longer harassed by sacristan kings; it was simply ignored.

In this order of things religious Orders had little or no meaning. The Catholic monarchs denied them contact with superiors in Rome or elsewhere outside their native countries and then set about "reforming" them, setting the age of profession, forbidding the acceptance of novices, prescribing the curriculum of studies, overseeing canonical elections and chapters, suppressing "useless" houses. These last inevitably included monasteries of contemplative nuns. Napoleon, following the principles of the French Revolution, simply suppressed religious Orders out of hand, as did the liberal governments of the 19th century, by the second half of which, with one or two exceptions, there remained only a few Carmelite nunneries in Italy and Spain.

Given the autonomous nature of Carmelite monasteries, the fate of cloistered Carmel at this time

112

Mary of the Patronage of St. Joseph, 1903-1936,
victim of the Spanish Civil War.

The cloister of the monastery of Saint Stephen,
Ravenna - Italy.
Photo by Riccardo Palazzi.

can be traced only in general outline. Each monastery has its own story of heroic sacrifice and tragedy, preserved only in individual archives. In the represent state of knowledge only the following fragmentary account is possible.

In Eastern Europe Carmel suffered severe losses under Emperor Joseph II (1780-1790). In 1781 he suppressed all establishments of religious men and women not dedicated to teaching, care of the sick, or scholarship. This edict marked the end of the province of Bohemia-Hungary-Austria, its eight convents and 202 members. The Order had no monasteries of nuns in these regions, but they did have them in the Spanish Netherlands, which had come into the possession of Austria in 1713. As a result, "useless" religious houses, especially of contemplatives, were also eliminated here (1783). The Carmelites lost the monasteries of Bruges, Louvain, Namur, and Marche. Guelders in the County of that name escaped, as did Boxmeer in Protestant Northern Provinces. Vilvoorde continued to exist, perhaps because the nuns had undertaken the education of girls.

The nunnery in Lwów was lost when Austria took over Galicia in the First Partition of Poland (1772).

In Italy the Order suffered much from the interference of secular authorities, especially in Milan and Tuscany, where the brothers of Emperor Joseph II ruled, but the monasteries of nuns for the time being survived. Pope Pius VI at the request of King Victor Amadeus of Savoy in 1783 suppressed the Mantuan Congregation and united its convents to the Order. The nunneries of the Congregation were placed in the care of the Piedmont province.

In 1755 occurred the horrendous earthquake of Lisbon, a disaster which devastated not only that city but extensive areas of Portugal itself and filled all Europe with fear and foreboding. On the morning of All Saints of that year, when the churches were crowded with the faithful fulfilling their holy day obligation, three heavy shocks over a period of five or six minutes reduced the city to a ruin under a thick cloud of dust. Shortly thereafter the sea rose in a great tidal wave, and the Tagus broke its banks, enveloping buildings and drowning their occupants. Even so, much might have been saved from the rubble, but a fierce fire broke out and utterly consumed the contents of public buildings, churches, palaces, libraries and archives of that wealthy and cultured city. It has been estimated that about ten to fifteen thousand persons were drowned, crushed, burnt, and otherwise killed in the catastrophe.

With the exception of Evora and Moura all the Carmelite friaries were destroyed or damaged. The greatest loss of all was the historic Carmo of Lisbon, tomb of Bl. Nuno Alvares Pereira. Today its gaunt and fragmentary walls, become a national monument, lower down on the city, a witness to a glorious past and its fiery ending.

At the time of the quake the provincial, Joseph of St. Anne Pereira, was visitating the nunnery in Lagos in Algarve, one of the areas hardest hit by the quake. The monastery, "a noble edifice," came crashing down, killing twenty-two nuns and severely injuring forty-three more, out of a community of one hundred and twenty-five, besides boarders and servants, three hundred persons in all. Pereira was saved by a wall left partially standing. Here as in Lisbon the sea rose to add to the damage and toll in lives. With his companions and the domestics the provincial set about extracting the nuns trapped in the ruins, saw to the burial of the dead and the care of the injured, and foraged for food, which was also shared with the poor. He managed to rescue the Blessed Sacrament buried under heaps of plaster and stone. For a week the friars and sisters had "no other shelter than a field under the open sky," Later Pereira was able to obtain shelter for the nuns.

The French Revolution swept away eight provinces of the Order with 721 members, actually only a remnant of former numbers. In 1789 the National Assembly confiscated the property of the Church, including that of religious Orders. The following

114

year it abolished vows and offered religious their freedom and a pension. The same year, 1790, it promulgated the Civil Constitution of the Clergy, eventually condemned by Pius VI, and imposed it on priests under oath. By 1782 the oath had become one of "Liberty and Equality," and carried the sanction of deportation or death. Estimates of the number of priests killed during the Terror range from 2,000 to 5,000. Deportation proved impracticable, due to the British blockade, so priests were crowded aboard slave ships in the estuary of the River Charante or on the islands off the coast of France.

As to the fate of the French Carmelites, some returned to their families or to private life. Those who were willing to take the oath were able to function as parish priests. Some Carmelites embraced the revolution, others joined the ranks of the *emigrés*. Finally some gave their lives for the faith.

Thirty-four Carmelite friars are known to have suffered death or imprisonment, but the last word has by no means been spoken on the Carmelites during the Revolution. Three were guillotined, best known among them the aged Martinien Pannetier (1718-1794), who before his capture managed to place in safety the relics of St. Simon Stock preserved in the Carmelite church in Bordeaux.

One of the most dramatic incidents during the Terror, celebrated in music, drama, and fiction, is the martyrdom by the guillotine in Paris of the sixteen Discalced Carmelite nuns of Compiègne. No nuns of the old Carmel are known to have been guillotined. They counted only six monasteries in the territory of France, but if one were to trace the history of their disappearance, one would no doubt encounter many examples of courageous Christian witness.

On June 1, 1790, the thirty-two nuns of "Les Couëts," in Nantes were expelled from their monastery by a crowd of men and women, among whom the president of the "Society of Patriotic Women" distinguished herself. The nuns are said to have been beaten on the occasion, and one of them thrown into a pond. They were able to return in December, but definitely left on August 26, 1792.

The prioress, Jeanne de La Roussière, and another nun were banished from the Republic. Another sister later died in the drownings at Nantes.

The monasteries of Nantes, Vannes, Rennes, and Ploërmel were in the care of the province of Touraine. The province of Francia had six monasteries under its jurisdiction, but only Charleville and Fumay, in the diocese of Reims, lay within the boundaries of France. After the suppression of the monasteries there, the vicariate of Liège took under its wing the four remaining monasteries of Liège, Huy, Dinant, and Rochefort, which thus received a few years' reprieve before being in turn suppressed.

After the dissolution of their monasteries women religious had no other alternative than to return to their families. Some Carmelites probably found asylum in exile.

In Belgium the French, on November 5, 1796, expelled the nuns from their monastery in Vilvoorde. Two weeks previously however Sister Petronilla of St. Mary had smuggled out the cherished statue of Our Lady of Consolation in a bale of hay, as one of her sisters had once done before her. Most of the nuns with the confessors of the monastery took refuge in the beguinage of the city, until the times permitted them to return on November 8, 1802. Their confessors were the exclaustrated Carmelites Cornelius Claes and Dionysius de Roey. With the establishment of modern Belgium in 1830 the nuns were once more free to accept novices. After thirty-four years only six nuns remained. The prioress was Joan Frances of St. Mary Vereecken.

Napoleon's rule over Europe was brief, but had disastrous and lasting effects on the Church and on religious Orders in particular. His policy was the outright dissolution of religious life. His impact on Carmel was especially felt in Germany and Italy.

The separate peace of Lunéville, 1801, between France and Austria ceded the left bank of the Rhine to France and compensated the losses of the German princes with the ecclesiastical states and free imperial cities on the right bank. In 1803 the property of religious Orders was declared forfeit.

These years saw the extinction of what was left of the Order in Germany: the 16 friaries of the Lower German province, the 6 friaries of the Upper German province, the 2 friaries of the Bavarian vicariate, and the 4 friaries of the Silesian vicariate. The nunnery of Guelders in the Lower German province shared the fate of the friary there.

When Napoleon incorporated The Netherlands into the empire, the religious houses were suppressed, 1812. Boxmeer fell under this edict, but by 1814 both friars and nuns were back in their respective houses. The ban on novices, however, remained in effect.

The monastery of Mount St. Mary in Cologne was suppressed in 1802. In 1763 the community numbered twenty-one sisters. They used double saints' names, so the monastery must have belonged to the Stricter Observance like the Lower German province of the friars, in which it was situated.

In Eastern Europe, after the Second and Third Partitions of Poland (1792, 1795), the Carmelite convents in Russian Poland were eliminated by the czars in the course of the 19th century. Only the six friaries in Austrian Galicia, with Cracow and Obory, remained in those parts. The nunnery of Dubno disappeared at this time, but as late as 1922 the property belonged to the Polish province.

The rule of Napoleon over Italy proved equally fatal to the Carmelites there. The general law of 1810 suppressed religious Orders throughout Italy. In northern Italy the provinces of Piedmont, Venice, Tuscany, and the vicariate of Genova succumbed. After Napoleon's fall the Tuscan province and, in the Papal States, the provinces of Romagna and Rome were revived, mere shadows of their former selves, In the Kingdom of Naples, the provinces of Puglia, Calabria, Terra di Lavoro, Naples, Santa Maria della Vita, and Abruzzo fell victim to the decree of Joachim Murat in 1809. After the restoration of the Bourbons it became possible to erect a new Neapolitan province with seven houses left over from the former provinces (1847). The province of Sardegna and the four Sicilian provinces were spared because they were protected by the British fleet.

The French occupation of Italy had the same deleterious effect on the Carmelite nunneries. Few of the thirty-odd foundations on the peninsula saw the second decade of the 19th century.

The nuns of St. Mary of the Angels in Florence were ejected from their home by the French, but were able to return afterwards. Already in 1786 they had provided asylum for their sisters of the Annunciation monastery, suppressed by Archduke Peter Leopold. Pisa, also in Tuscany, and Pescia in Lucca probably were extinguished at this time.

The monasteries in the north were all lost: Asti (the Presentation and the Holy Family) in Piedmont, Pontecurone in Lombardy, and the four nunneries of the Venetian group: Venice (St. Teresa), Padua, Verona, and Vicenza. A community of *pinzocchere* in Venice, the conservatory of Our Lady of Hope, ended its three hundred-year existence.

In the Papal States the *Barberine* of Rome outlived the troubles of the 19th century, but subsequently left the eternal city to return to their mother house in Florence (1907). Of the two foundations made from this monastery, Vetralla and Monterotonda, the former flourishes today. Iesi in the Marches also defied all attempts on its life and in 1882 welcomed the refugees from Montecarotto. Orvieto in Umbria fell a victim to the war on nuns.

Of ten monasteries in the Kingdom of Naples, that of the Holy Cross in Naples, which provided a home for their sisters of the monastery of the Blessed Sacrament, Castellamare (Holy Cross), and Solofra remained intact. Avellino, Castellamare (St. Teresa), Caulonia, Montecorvino, Putignano, and Somma succumbed to the pressures of the times.

The Sicilian nunneries, like the friaries, for the time being were safe.

The bull of suppression of 1783, as we have seen, placed the nuns of the Mantuan Congregation in the care of the Piedmont province. Jerome Vigo, writing not long after 1783, lists only six nunneries: Albino, Brescia, Florence (St. Barnabas), Novellara, Reggio, and Trino. He also includes Mantua, but himself chronicles its suppression, June 29, 1782. The other seven monasteries—Parma, Bologna (*" conver-*

tite "), Bergamo, Camaiore, and the three foundations of the Congregation in Ferrara—had evidently already undergone the fate of the friaries. In any case there is no evidence that they survived the French occupation. In the Papal States, Sutri and Velletri, not mentioned by Vigo, staunchly resisted extinction—Velletri until 1921, Sutri until the present day.

Thus in the end the numerous nunneries of Italy had been reduced to fourteen: Florence, Rome (-1907), Velletri (-1921), Sutri, Vetralla, Iesi, Ostuni, Naples, Castellamare (-1952), Solofra (-1939), Fisciano, Messina, Palermo, Siracusa.

Oddly enough, in these calamitous years the Order actually acquired a monastery. Anna of St. Teresa, a Carmelite tertiary of Molinella (Bologna) under the direction of Fr. Peter Tombi, had for years lived in retirement, dedicated to prayer and good works. By 1773 others had joined her, and a community was formed, which that same year transferred to Ravenna. The Sisters devoted themselves to the education of girls and the care of the aged. In 1782, according to the new disposition of the Congregation of Bishops and Religious, the community as a diocesan congregation passed under the jurisdiction of the bishop. After dispersal by the French the community regrouped, but the Carmelite friary of Ravenna did not revive, and the Sisters lost contact with the Order. In 1840 they undertook papal cloister and solemn vows. They professed the Carmelite rule as mitigated by Pope Eugene IV and followed constitutions revised by their ecclesiastical superior, Cardinal Chiarissimo Confalieri.

In Spain, Joseph Bonaparte's brief reign, mostly preoccupied with the Peninsular War, had no lasting effect on religious life, though the invader left behind him his usual traces of destruction and rapine. A wing of the monastery of Aracena was destroyed by fire and its archive lost.

The monastery of Las Maravillas lay in the center of the fighting during the insurrection against the French on May 2, 1808. The nuns were frightened out of their wits by the rain of cannon shot that fell on their monastery, but one courageous novice, Edwarda of St. Bonaventure, crawled out a window and with crucifix in hand went about among the soldiers to raise their spirits, an incident remembered by more than one historian. After the chaplain calmed their fears the sisters took on the care of the wounded without regard to friend or foe. One young French officer had the consolation of hearing his native tongue spoken by the nun who assisted him at his last moments on earth. She was Sister Pelagia Revult, who entered the monastery in 1794, possibly an emigrée during the revolution.

In the 19th century liberal governments, as secular States, carried forward the dissolution of religious Orders. As far as the Carmelite nuns is concerned, apart from Boxmeer and Vilvoorde, only the monasteries of Spain, Portugal, were involved.

In Spain the century was occupied by the long struggle between the monarchy and republicanism, ending only with the abdication of Alphonse XIII in 1931. Although except for brief intervals a king or queen was on the throne, the republican element often controlled the Cortes and managed to make their policies prevail. These changes did not always take place without violence.

The final suppression of religious Orders occurred in 1836 under the prime minister Juan Alvarez Mendizábal. His decree of March 8 effectively eliminated the Carmelite provinces of Catalonia, Aragon, Castile, and Andalusia. The friars returned to their families or became diocesan priests. Few are known to have emigrated. Religious Orders were again re-instated in 1851, but the Carmelites did not return until the end of the century.

The law of 1836 was more lenient on the nuns. Leaving unaffected the sisters engaged in teaching and nursing, the law suppressed all monasteries of cloistered nuns with less than twenty members. However these smaller communities were allowed to join those which qualified for continued existence. Only one monastery of an Order was allowed in each town. The sisters were forbidden to accept novices, and their property was sequestered, thus withdrawing their means of support. The law of exclaustration, or the so-called right of religious to secularize, was also affirmed. Much to the disappointment of the liberals the nuns showed no great inclination to avail themselves of the proffered freedom. Quite the contrary. They raised such a holy dust with the queen that their affairs were conducted with considerable leniency by diocesan committees and other authorities. The seizure of their property worked great hardship on cloistered women, but they asked only to be allowed to die in peace in their beloved cloisters. It should have occurred to the apostles of liberty that in denying these women their desire to live their own innocent lives they were trampling on some rather fundamental human rights.

As a result of the stiff resistance of the nuns only about 150 to 200 of 1000 to 1070 monasteries underwent amalgamation. When the ban on novices was lifted in 1851, the nuns were back in business.

The story of the Carmelite nuns in Spain corresponds to the general situation.

On the eve of the exclaustration the Order in Spain still had its full complement of twenty-six monasteries; in the province of Castile: Madrid (Las Maravillas), Madrid (La Baronesa), Avila, Fontiveros, Piedrahita; in Catalonia: Barcelona, Villafranca del Panadés, Valls, Vich; in Aragon: Valencia (Incarnation), Valencia (St. Anne), Onteniente, Sariñena, Huesca (Incarnation), Huesca (Assumption), Zaragoza; in Andalusia; Ecija, Granada, Seville (Incarnation), Seville (St. Anne), Antequera, Aracena, Osuna, Utrera, Villalba del Alcor, Cañete La Real.

In most cities with two Carmelite monasteries, one was eliminated. In Madrid the nuns of La Baronesa joined their sisters in Las Maravillas, bringing with them their precious autograph of St. Teresa and other articles of devotion, including busts of Christ crowned with thorns and of the Sorrowful Mother, attributed to Pedro de Mena and José de Mora. In 1869 this community was also turned out of doors to find shelter with the Mercedarians until 1891, when it once again acquired its old home. Twice the nuns were victims of fraud by administrators of their funds. The sort of individual who will defraud a community of cloistered women is low indeed on the roster of confidence men.

In Valencia the monastery of St. Anne was amalgamated to the Incarnation, in Seville the monastery of St. Anne took in the Incarnation. In 1852 Ecija was united to Osuna. Sariñena seems to have been simply suppressed outright. In 1842 the Assumption in Huesca was united to the Incarnation, but the nuns were able to return to their original home in 1852. Again in 1868 they were expelled, only to return once more. By 1888 there were only three nuns left in Utrera, but reinforcements from Granada gave them a new lease on life.

Thus in spite of bullying and force the Carmelite nuns persevered in their hidden life of prayer, though in slightly fewer monasteries. They may be confidently included in the praise which Revuelta González, sober historian of the exclaustration, lavishes on all Spanish nuns: "the protagonists in one of the most admirable and unheralded demonstrations of faith in contemporary history."

Spain was anticipated by Portugal in the matter of suppressing religious Orders. The law of 1834 dissolved the fourteen Carmelite friaries of the Portuguese province. The bankrupt government was in no position nor mood to lavish generous pensions on the dispossessed religious. Their plight in Portugal seems to have been more critical than elsewhere. In 1842 a visiting prince was struck by "the thousands of friars, suddenly cast upon the world with such meager means of subsistence that an ex-religious and beggar appear to be almost synonymous."

The nuns were allowed to remain in their monasteries as long as they lived, but were forbidden to accept novices. The Order had four nunneries in Portugal: Beja, Lagos, Tentúgal, and Guimarães. In 1846 the Carmelites of Beja took in the Poor Clares. In 1894, the last prioress, Maria José Segurado, was elected the ninth time. After her death the church was torn down by the Viscount of Ribeira Brava, who transported certain of its furnishings to his property in Vidigueira. A modern building, completed in 1940, replaces the monastery.

The last surviving sister in Tentúgal, the *Revista carmelitana* reports under the date line, July 23, 1889, is seventy-seven years old and ill. When she dies, the government will impound church and monastery.

In Italy the *Risorgimento,* or unification of the traditional political units of the peninsula and islands under the crown of Savoy, marked the final dissolution of the religious Orders there. In 1866 religious Orders were abolished and their property sequestered in the Kingdom of Italy. In 1873, after the annexation of the Papal States, the law was applied there. Thus perished whatever was left of the Order: the provinces of Sardegna, Tuscany, Romagna, Roma, Naples, and the Sicilian provinces of St. Angelus, Monte Santo, and Santa Maria della Scala. However one or two Carmelites were usually left in charge of the church, and from these nuclei was to arise the Carmel of today. Only in 1929 did the Lateran Pact recognize the legal existence of religious Orders.

Nuns were allowed to occupy their monasteries until their death, or if the government had need of their buildings, they were moved in with other communities. In Rome, the Ministry of War sequestered the Carmelite monastery. With the Cappucin nuns, the Carmelites joined the Canonesses of the Lateran. They suffered this arrangement until 1907, when they returned to their original home, St. Mary of the Angels, Florence. In 1899, the government moved the Carmelites from the monastery of the Holy Cross in Naples to a former religious house, "La Maddalenella."

Each monastery will have its own story to tell of those difficult years. Only the Sicilian monasteries of Messina, Palermo failed to revive. The monastery of St. Lucy of Valverde in Palermo was still at hand in 1892, when the sisters begged the penniless prior general for financial assistance. The beautiful church remains today.

To sum up the disastrous century, 1750-1850, around the year 1875 there remained forty monasteries of cloistered Carmelites: in the Low Countries 2 (Boxmeer, Vilvoorde), Italy 13, Spain 21,

Portugal 4. The four Portuguese monasteries, forbidden to receive novices, did not survive the 19th century. In Spain the war on the nuns resulted in only five casualties: Madrid (La Baronesa), Valencia (St. Anne), Ecija, Sariñena, and Seville (Incarnation).

In spite of the weight of public opinion against them and even of active persecution by governments, women with a contemplative vocation quietly continued to follow their bent. If in the best of times they are not given to vaunting their accomplishments, it need hardly be said that information regarding the period under consideration is of the scantiest. A few examples of cloistered Carmelite nuns may be offered here.

Sister Mary Magdalen Gertrude (1775-1807) united in her veins the noble blood of the Corsinis and Barberinis. As a child she was given into the custody of her aunt, Sister Anne Constance Barberini, a nun in the Dominican monastery of St. Catherine of Siena in Rome. Even after the family moved to Florence she hoped to return and enter this monastery, but her parents would not consent to such a separation. Nevertheless the young girl persisted in her desire to become a nun and entered the Carmelite monastery of Our Lady of the Angels in Florence. There she was put in charge of temporal administration, an office that suited her peculiar gifts. From her girlhood Mary Magdalen had been known for her down-to-earth practical sense. She now pressed and brought to a successful issue the beatifcation of the Dominican Maria Bartolomea Bagnesi, whose body was buried in the Carmelite monastery. The many letters to influential persons, not excluding the pope, which she wrote in this cause, show a not indifferent talent for clear, smoothly flowing prose. She wrote a *Compendio* of Bagnesi's life, published in Parma, but her other writings she burned out of humility. This virtue was one of the outstanding features of the young noblewoman's spirit. Others were her serenity, uprightness, and good judgement. At her early death at the age of thirty-two she had already distinguished herself as a religious of more than ordinary goodness.

Also from the monastery of St. Mary of the Angels in Florence was Mary Magdalen Constance of the Blessed Sacrament Picchi (1839-1895). She came from a well-to-do Florentine family, her father being a music master. Her mother, née Virginia Bargigli, died in 1854. Her father was not opposed to her religious vocation, but would not hear of her entering a strict contemplative community. After his death however, being free to follow her natural inclination, she chose the Carmelite monastery of St. Mary of the Angels in Florence, where she entered the novitiate on February 15, 1859. She had to wait ten years to pronounce her vows, because the Tuscan government had decided that nuns should not make profession until they were thirty years of age. With the suppression of 1866 their future became even more uncertain, their monastery being sequestered and available for their use only for their lifetime. Under the circumstances the archbishop of Florence, Joachim Limberti, permitted the nuns to make only simple profession, which Mary Magdalen Constance finally made on May 13, 1872. Upon the accession of Archbishop Eugene Cesconi and better times she was allowed to make solemn profession on June 4, 1876. Mary Magdalen Constance served in all the offices of the monastery: assistant novice mistress, bursar (during the move to the Piazza Savonarola in 1888), novice mistress, prioress. In all these capacities she comported herself with a perfection which convinced her sisters of her extraordinary virtue. She left a spiritual diary published after her death by her director, Alexander Gallerani, S. J., as well as biographies of several sisters who had been under her care in the novitiate.

One of these was Frances Teresa of the Holy Angels Giovannini (1837-1903), whose life was likewise written by Fr. Gallerani. She was remarkable for her continual state of prayer, abandonment to to the will of God, and humility.

Sister Mary Minima Louise of Jesus of Nazareth Salvatori (1730-1831) was one of those persons who from infancy show an inclination to prayer and an

aptitude for mystical gifts. She was born in Capra-
rola near Rome, of a family that seems to have been
well provided with this world's goods. From the
ages of eight to twelve she attended the school of
St. John in Zoccoli in Viterbo, conducted by the
Maestre Pie, one of whom was the inevitable aunt.
In what she later considered a lapse from grace she
began a courtship with a young man, but her celibate calling reasserted itself, and she entered the
Carmelite monastery in Vetralla, pronouncing her
vows on June 7, 1804. The suppression of the monasteries in 1810 found her back in her family. There
as much as possible she led the life of a cloistered
nun. The sisters had been instructed to apply to
their confessors for the permissions they would
normally seek from the prioress. She had the good
fortune to find an excellent spiritual director in the
Discalced Carmelite, Paul of St. Joseph, who was
her guide in the ways of the spirit for the rest of
her days. After the return of Pius VIII, Vetralla
was not immediately ready to receive its inmates,
but Mary Minima in November of 1814 was taken
in by the *Barberine* in Rome, until she was able to
return to her own monastery on September 29, 1819.
From 1822 until her death she was prioress, being
re-elected to that office three times. Her special
effort was to repair the spiritual and material damage done by the suppression. Fr. Paul had ordered
Sister Mary Minima to record her spiritual itinerary
in writing, and this document at once served him
in composing her biography (Roma, 1833) and also
shows her to have practiced the most heroic virtues
and to have reached the most exalted mystical
states.

At the age of twelve Sister Mary Emilia Gutta-
dauro (1829-1877) entered the monastery of the Holy
Cross in Naples as an *educanda*. Her religious life
was characterized by obedience. She accepted with
serenity whatever her superiors or divine Providence
had in store for her. No doubt this attitude had its
origin in her relation to her aunt, Sister Mary Rosa
Ricciardi, to whom as a child she was wholly submissive; yet her conformity took the form of a
loving attachment rather than a grovelling ser-

vitude. Sister Mary Emilia made her profession on October 25, 1853. During her religious life she held only the humbler offices, such as assistant sacristan, portress, baker, assistant directress of the *educande*. Only months before her death she became sub-prioress. A striking feature of her life were the amazing mystical phenomena which together with continual illness occurred therein. On April 26, 1856, she was cured of total paralysis and blindness through a vision of Our Lady of Good Counsel. This event was the prelude to a lifetime of visions and raptures. Of these sensational manifestations it may at least be said that they left behind in her solid fruits of virtue. "Her virtue," wrote Sister Mary Matilda Buonanno, her companion and biographer, "was a lovable and tender virtue... It was a happy virtue, not narrowminded, always in good taste, compliant."

If the Carmelite monastery of Osuna exists today, it is due in no slight measure to Sister Mary Josefa of the Incarnation Amarillo (1811-1891). Born in the town of Arahal, she early manifested a desire to become a religious, but she lacked the means to provide her dowry. Since she could play the organ, the Sisters waived this condition, and Sister Mary Josefa received the habit on July 1, 1827. At the time, the community counted only seven nuns, but this number must have soon increased, for the monastery survived the suppression of small communities in 1836. In 1852, as we have seen, the community was joined by that of Ecija. For thirty-three years until her death Sister Mary Josefa headed the monastery as prioress and brought about its spiritual and material renewal. A new church, blessed on April 29, 1883, replaced the old structure which threatened ruin. She also renovated the monastery. More important than these material improvements, necessary though they were, she re-instated the common life. Shortly before her death she had the consolation of seeing her brothers in Carmel return to Osuna consequent on her effective intervention and fervent prayers.

Similarly, Sister Mary Teresa Falangola (1835-1908) was gratefully remembered by the sisters of the Carmel of Castellamare for her devotion to the contemplative vocation and her zeal for the house of the Lord. Born in Naples and baptised Antonietta, she was left an orphan at the age of nine. Thereupon she was placed in the Benedictine monastery of St. Paul, Sorrento, but after eleven years illness caused her to return to the home of her grandparents. Three years later she entered the Carmelite monastery of Our Lady of Peace in Castellamare. When this monastery was suppressed in 1868, Mary Teresa and a few other sisters took up residence in a private house, but she soon requested and was granted admittance to the Discalced Carmelite monastery in Chiaia. Meanwhile the Castellamare community had found a permanent abode in the *Cognulo* section of the city under the prioress Mary Louise, a sister of Mary Teresa. At the former's death, the bishop recalled Mary Teresa from Chiaia to head the community. Since the Italian government had confiscated the nuns' dowries the monastery was in dire financial straits. It was Mary Teresa's task and accomplishment to guide the monastery through these difficult years to more prosperous days.

Josephine Koning, 1863-1931,
of the monastery of St. Joseph, Boxmeer - The Netherlands.
Painting by Pieter Geraedts.

A Sister at prayer. Carmel of St. Anne,
Carpineto Romano - Italy

Chapter VII

CLOISTERED CARMEL RESTORED

The scorn of the Enlightenment and the open hostility of 19th century Liberalism effected a blight on cloistered Carmelite life that lasted two and a half centuries. The active sisterhoods were found socially useful, and this was the period of their origin and growth, Carmelite sisterhoods as well, but the 18th century saw only the foundation of Ostuni (1730). Sister Carmela Montalto's conservatory in Siracusa achieved cloister in 1738. If Montecorvino (1766) was a cloistered monastery, it had only a brief existence.

In all of the 19th century only two foundations were made: these in the Netherlands, where the friars were making a comeback. When the ban on novices was lifted in 1840, new candidates quickly presented themselves in the monastery of Elzendaal in Boxmeer. With the arrival of the Sisters of Charity in 1865, the Carmelites were able to discontinue teaching, a task, we have seen, formerly imposed on them by the exigencies of the times.

By 1870 the community numbered fifty nuns, and Elzendaal could give thought to founding another monastery. The provincial, Augustine Van Uden, conducted ten sisters, led by the prioress, Mother Ignatia Koeken, from Boxmeer to Xanten in the diocese of Munster and on May 19, 1870, solemnly inaugurated the monastery. Fr. Dionysius Wellessen, accompanied by a laybrother, remained behind as confessor. The prior general, Angelo Savini, did not overlook this infant Carmel during his visitation of 1871. "We have great hopes for this foundation," he noted. The Iron Chancellor had other ideas. In 1875 the Xanten community, a fugitive from the *Kulturkampf*, again presented itself in Boxmeer. A home was found for the sisters in Boxmeer itself, in the monastery of St. Joseph, initiated on May 16, 1876.

In 1888 the bees of Elzendaal were again ready to swarm, by no means the last time. On May 23, 1889, twelve nuns began a new Carmel in Zenderen.

During the first decades of the present century, too, growth remained practically at a standstill. The famous Father John Baptist Felíu founded the Carmel of Caudete with nuns from Onteniente, headed by his sister, Joachima of Jesus (1914). "Elzendaal" in Boxmeer gave rise to Heerlen in 1928. Sister Therese of Jesus crossed the seas from Naples to found the monastery of Allentown, Pa. (1931).

On the other hand, some of the existing monasteries, as we have seen, ceased to be at this time: Rome (1907), Velletri (1921), Solofra (1939), and Castellamare (1952).

While the restoration of the male branch of the Order had already begun in the late 1800's, the nuns did not recover until the second half of the present century. A feature of the revival of the friars was a re-awakening of concern for their sisters. Thought was given to their organization and centralization on a world-wide basis. In 1925 the office of commissary general for the nuns was instituted in the person of Spiridion Varsallo, second assistant general. At the same time it was decided to draw up uniform legislation for all Carmelite monasteries in conformity with the new code of canon law, which had appeared in 1918. However, it was only a decade later that the constitutions were completed by Manuel Baranera Serra and approved by the Sacred Congregation of Religious on the feast of Our Lady of Mount Carmel, July 16, 1935. Translations appeared in Dutch, Italian, and Spanish, all in 1936, and in English in 1938. The constitutions were accepted by all the Carmelite monasteries except St. Mary of the Angels (by that time moved from Florence to Careggi), which had its own constitutions approved by the Holy See in 1936. Thus a major obstacle to the development of Carmel's cloistered life, the isolation of the monasteries, was largely overcome, and the modern period of its history may be said to have begun.

No doubt the delayed revival of cloistered Carmel was influenced by the civil war in Spain, which at the time was becoming one of the most flourishing parts of the Order, where two provinces and a commissariate, totalling 245 members, had already been re-constituted.

The civil war, 1936-1939, cost the Church, besides incalculable material loss in the destruction of ecclesiastical property, the lives of 4,184 diocesan priests, 2,365 religious men, and 283 religious women. Among these were 57 Carmelite friars (counting 3 missing after the war) and 4 Carmelite nuns. The 4 convents of the new Catalan province were destroyed, and 16 friars killed. Five of the 7 convents of the Arago-Valentina province suffered from the war, and 28 friars killed. Of the 8 convents of the Andalusian province, 2 were damaged, and 10 friars killed.

The Spanish nunneries in the loyalist zone where extreme leftists were in control were likewise not spared, although information about their fate is at present rather fragmentary. In most cases the sisters were probably forced to abandon their monasteries and seek shelter among families, friends, other monasteries, or even foreign countries.

The four Catalan monasteries (Barcelona, Villafranca del Pañadés, Vich, and Valls) suffered complete or partial destruction. Two nuns from Villafranca found a temporary home in Heerlen, others returned to their families or friends and were sometimes able to be of assistance to priests in hiding.

The Barcelona nuns had already seen their monastery devastated during the anarchist revolt in July, 1909, known as the "Tragic Week." Now again on July 19, 1936, the twenty-seven nuns were forced to abandon their cloister and seek shelter in private homes. Fifteen of them were aboard the "Sicilia" which sailed for Italy on September 10 with a thousand nuns. Fr. Albert Grammatico was on hand in Genoa to conduct the sisters to Rome. They were welcomed in monasteries in Florence, Jesi, Vetralla, and Rome, until they were able to return to Barcelona in 1939. The monastery had been used as a prison and was substantially intact, though in need of extensive repairs. The furnishings of the church had been burned.

In Catalonia there was also a community of tertiary sisters in Bañoles. Founded in 1858 by Carmen of St. John of the Cross, a refugee from the 1848 revolution in Rome, it was affiliated with the Order in 1907. Only in 1951 did the sisters obtain the status of cloistered nuns of the Order. Their monastery was spared destruction in 1936, but required renovation before it was again habitable.

Elsewhere, in Caudete (founded in 1915) the nuns had already been expelled in the revolution of 1931. During the Civil War they were again made to abandon their monastery, which with the church they found in ruins on their return. The church of the Incarnation monastery in Huesca was hit by an incendiary bomb. The nuns were reciting the liturgical hours, but escaped without injury. The monastery of the Assumption in the same town was also destroyed, as was Onteniente.

The monastery and church of Cañete la Real were sacked and their furnishings burned or stolen. The nuns at first were taken in by friends but were later expelled from the town. They took refuge in the monasteries of Osuna, Jerez de la Frontera, and Seville (S. Ana). Toward the end of their exile they were able to gather together as a community.

In Utrera Sister Natividad Aranda who lay dying at thirty-five years of age offered her life for the safety of her sisters. She died on July 14, and in fact the sisters remained unharmed.

The community of Madrid (Las Maravillas) was also forced to leave the monastery briefly in the revolution of 1931. In the Civil War church and convent were damaged by fire, the nuns dispersed. Afterwards they gathered in an apartment in the Calle Ayala 127 until their monastery could be restored. The church was finished in 1942.

Four Carmelite nuns lost their lives. Mary of the Patronage of St. Joseph Badía Flaquer (1903-1936), of the monastery of Vich, on an errand to neighbors, unfortunately arrived while a search of the premises was in progress. With the others in the house she was taken to the town hall for questioning. Her youth and attractiveness were the cause for additional harassment. About 11 o'clock at night on August 13 she was driven in a car with four soldiers to San Martín de Ruideperas. A second car held the eighty-nine year-old vicar general of the diocese, James Serra Jordi, and the pastor of Artés, Joseph Bisbal. The cars stopped at the parish church and the priests were taken out and shot. Sister Mary tried to run away, but was shot down with machine guns.

Sister Trinity Martínez Gil (1893-1936), sub-prioress of the Incarnation in Valencia, went into hiding in her native Alcudia de Carlet. She was taken into custody with another woman whom she never ceased to comfort as they were taken to the place of their execution on the road to Sueca, September 24.

Sister Josepha Ricard Casabant (1889-1936), of the same monastery, was executed in her native Albal on the road to Silla, September 8. She was killed together with the parish priest of the town, whose death she was forced to witness before being told that it was now her turn.

A victim belonging to the Incarnation of Barcelona was Dolores of St. John of the Cross, aged 61.

On the heels of the Spanish civil war came World War II (1939-1945). It was the turn of the Dutch and Italian nuns to suffer. Ravenna and Vetralla were destroyed in aerial raids. Even when the monasteries were spared material loss, religious routine was disrupted and recollection disturbed, when the sisters had to leave the cloister in areas under fire. On their return they hardly found their homes as they had left them. Again, each monastery has its own story to tell of those parlous times.

In the generalate of Kilian Lynch, and due largely to his interest, cloistered Carmel came to life again. In 1948 "Elzendaal" in Boxmeer joined Heerlen to form a community in Jaboticabal, Brazil. Eight years later "Elzendaal" founded the first monastery of the old Carmel in England at Blackburn, Lancashire (1956). Not to be outdone, St. Joseph's in Boxmeer in 1948 established at Schlüsselau the first German cloistered Carmel since that of Cologne (1565-1802). In 1958 it also made a foundation in Oss.

In Spain "Las Maravillas" of Madrid founded the Carmel of San José de las Matas, Dominican Republic (1954). Four years later it established the first cloistered Carmel in the Far East at Dumaguete in the Philippine Islands. Seville undertook the return of the Carmelite nuns to Portugal, making foundations at Moncorvo (1949) and Beja (1954). In 1955 Utrera and Villalba joined forces to found the first African Carmelite monastery at Kakamega, Kenya. Barcelona and Villafranca del Pañadés together added a sixth Catalan monastery in Tárrega (1953). In 1951 the sisters of Bañolas had accepted cloister to become the fifth Catalan monastery. The same year the Third Order sisters of Camerino in Italy had become cloistered nuns.

In the United States, Allentown gave rise to Wahpeton, N.D. (1954) and Asheville, N.C. (1956). The first Carmelite monastery in the New World, San Juan in Puerto Rico, which at the time had moved to Santurce, P. R., established another Caribbean Carmel at Ciudad Trujillo in the Dominican Republic (1957).

The interesting feature of this development is the way the sisters left familiar European haunts to introduce Carmelite contemplative life in lands beyond the seas.

Cloistered Carmel continues to teach women the way to divine intimacy. Among sisters remarkable for holiness might be mentioned Gesualda of the Holy Spirit (1879-1930), of St. Mary of the Angels, Florence; Josephine Koning (1863-1931), of St. Joseph's, Boxmeer; Elia of the Mother of God (1906-1934), of Vilvoorde; Rosaria of St. Philomena (1865-1935), of Ostuni; Therese of Jesus (1877-1939), of Allentown, Pa.; Mary Lourdes of the Most Blessed Sacrament (1916-1948), of Piedrahita; Mary Magdalen de' Pazzi Sanz Perea (1876-1953), of Utrera.

CONCLUSION

On this positive note we end this brief history of the Carmelite nuns. We conclude our story short of the Second Vatican Council. The effect of this momentous gathering on religious life has been keenly felt but cannot yet be adequately evaluated. The changes the council brought about in Catholic life have created an initial crisis in religious Orders, manifesting itself particularly in a drastic diminution of vocations, but as soon as the vibrant new spirituality has taken a deeper hold, we may be sure that young people will again be drawn to the contemplative life in renewed Orders. The history of the Church shows that religious life, active and contemplative, for women as well as for men, is a spontaneous and perennial expression of Catholic faith.

This account has confined itself largely to external events in the life of cloistered Carmel, which is the author's particular competence, and has had little to say about its spirituality. Meanwhile the recital of Carmel's itinerary through the ages may be welcome to the sisters themselves and to others interested in the history of religious women. It may already be noted, perhaps, that the spirituality of the Carmelite nuns is no different than the friars', though it finds expression in greater interiority. Like that of other medieval Orders, Carmel's spirituality is not specific or different from Christian devotion in general; it is only its intensification. This is at once its weakness and its strength. The Carmelite nun and friar have no charismatic model or clearly defined life style to guide their daily actions. On the other hand they are less likely to become stagnated in the spirituality of a given age or a specific aspect of Christian life. They have been with the Church a long while. They are at home in the Church of any time and all times.

Appendix 1

THE CONGREGATION OF THE MOST HOLY SAVIOR

The guiding spirit of this movement was Seraphina of God, born Prudence Pisa of a wealthy Neapolitan merchant family. On her mother's side she was connected with the ancient Strina family of Capri. When Prudence was two years old, her father Nicholas, who had already fathered a family by a previous marriage, retired with his remaining children to his properties on Capri. Two of her uncles were in the Church, Ottavio Pisa, canon of the cathedral of Naples, and Marcello Strina, pastor of the cathedral parish of Capri. Her tutor from the age of nine was a Dominican tertiary, Sister Antonia, succeeded by another, Sister Ipolita, both of whom fostered her inclination to a life of prayer. During her teens Prudence herself wore the Dominican tertiary habit, in which she was clothed by her uncle, until forbidden to wear it by the bishop who thought Don Marcello was much too lenient in conferring this exacting obligation. A severe loss to Prudence was the death at eighteen of her sister Victoria, three years her junior and her confidante and collaborator in her religious aspirations. From the age of fourteen Prudence had a regular confessor, Antonio d'Arena, archdeacon of the cathedral of Capri and spiritual director of the family, including Don Marcello, who in turn undertook the direction of his niece on Don Antonio's death. Don Marcello was an ecclesiastic of more than ordinary dedication and enlisted his niece's spiritual energies on behalf of his dream to see founded on Capri a monastery of nuns, hitherto lacking. To this end he had already interested Prudence in the work of recruiting religious vocations and bequeathed her properties for the erection of the proposed monastery. He fell victim to the pestilence of 1656, as did his sister, Prudence's mother. Ottavio Pisa took his place as his niece's spiritual director.

Prudence was forty years old when she began her

activity as foundress. Until then she apparently lived the life of a *pinzocchera* in the midst of her family, devoting herself to prayer and good works.

To find candidates for her proposed monastery she returned to Naples. There she managed to recruit Prudence Favale who subsequently left for reasons of health, a Dominican tertiary Cecil Tedesco and her ward Christina Bucci, and two orphaned relatives, Teresa and Olympia Martorelli, who were in the care of Don Ottavio Pisa. On Capri they were joined by a native of the island Anna Alfano. It was in the Carmine Maggiore, on April 23, 1661, that Prudence received the inspiration to enroll her monastery in the ranks of Carmel.

Returning to the island with her brood, Prudence provisionally took up residence in a house placed at her disposal by a relative, Antonio di Leo. The formal introduction of the community into their dwelling took place with a solemn ceremony in the cathedral of St. Stephen, May 29, 1661. There too the vicar apostolic Horace d'Amato performed the clothing, so that the populace could witness the unprecedented ceremony. Don Ottavio preached. On October 2 the sisters were able to move into the house which had been bequeathed for the purpose by Don Marcello.

These premises too the community soon outgrew. This time the imposing church and monastery of the Most Holy Savior were constructed by the engineer Dionysius Lazzari and consecrated by Cardinal Vincent Orsini, October 11, 1675. In this work Sr. Prudence was assisted by her friend, the Oratorian Vincent Avinatri (*d.* 1685), who contributed generously from his private resources. He had undertaken her spiritual direction after the death of Ottavio Pisa (1672). For the high altar of the church he now contributed a painting of the Savior, a family heirloom, which was mounted over a large picture of the Holy Family by Luca Giordano. The nave was ornamented with paintings from the school of Solimene.

In 1672 the community initiated the practice of assuming religious names. Prudence took the name Seraphina of God. In selecting names for her daughters she showed an exuberant fantasy resulting in products wholly untranslatable.

138

By the time the new church and monastery on Capri were finished she had already made another foundation on the mainland. On October 4, 1673, the bishop of Capri, Francis Mary Neri, himself accompanied the foundress and three sisters to Massalubrense, where they were joined by nine candidates for the new foundation dedicated to St. Teresa.

At the invitation of the bishop of Vico Equense, John Baptist Repucci, Seraphina in 1676 crossed over with Sisters Diletta of Jesus and Avventurata of Mary and settled in the former Carmelite convent there. After two months twelve aspirants had joined her. In 1689 construction was begun on a new monastery dedicated to the Blessed Trinity and located on another site.

At Nocera de' Pagani on the other hand the foundress had to overcome the resistance of the bishop, Felix Gabrielli. The foundation had been urged by a priest, Matthew Angelus Scalfari, and a layman, John Leonard Unghero. A visit to the bishop however sufficed to win him over, in spite of the fact that he was suffering from an attack of the gout, and in 1680 Seraphina with three other sisters settled in a house contingent to the Church of Our Lady of the Martyrs. In 1684 the new monastery of Our Lady of Purity was begun, to which the Oratorians Charles Lombardi and Dominic Rinaldi contributed generously. Five years later the community numbered twenty-one sisters, six lay sisters and eight boarders.

St. Michael the Archangel was the patron saint of Anacapri, a saint for whom Seraphina also fostered a particular devotion. This circumstance and a vow made to the saint in the event of victory in the battle of Vienna of 1683 led her the same year to found a house in Anacapri. A wealthy gentleman, Anthony Migliacci, a Sardinian who spent his vacations on Capri, undertook to provide a church and monastery, but died before their completion. This consummation was brought about through the generosity of Bishop Michael Gallo Vandeinde. The floor of the octagonal church is occupied, wall to wall, with the magnificent ceramic by Leonardo Chiaiese, depicting the earthly paradise from designs by Solimene (1761). No more appropriate setting for such a theme than Capri. To Solimene are also attributed fifteen paintings in the church:

At the request of the archbishop of Naples, Cardinal Innico Caraccioli, Seraphina in 1685 carried out the reform of the Dominican conservatory in Torre del Greco, founded in 1656 by Sister Frances Malafronte. Her first step was to remove the institution from secular control and to place it under the jurisdiction of the bishop. Of the nineteen sisters, mostly Neapolitans, and eight laysisters Seraphina sent seven back to their families. The rest agreed to undertake the perfect common life and to accept the Carmelite habit and rule. The house was dedicated to the Immaculate Conception.

The foundation of the monastery of St. Joseph in Fisciano, which finally took place in 1691, was long delayed by litigation over the will of the wealthy Blaise Aversa who had bequeathed the property for this purpose. Seraphina did not personally supervise the foundation, but delegated Sr. Arcangela Fortunata.

The reason Seraphina did not personally found Fisciano was that from April 22, 1689, to October 9, 1691, she was confined to her cell without the Eucharist, while the Inquisition considered her case. She submitted without demur and in the end was declared innocent of whatever accusations had been brought against her. Those were the times of the hunt against Quietism in the Kingdom of Naples. Seraphina early recognized Molinos' prayer of faith for what it was and is said to have corresponded with him over the matter. Her brief tract on the prayer of faith has been printed. She wrote voluminously, but her writings, revealing her ardent and intensely human spirit, were never published. Their whereabouts, if they still exist, remains to be determined.

After her trial she made no more foundations and seems to have passed the last decade of her life on the island. For that matter she was already far advanced in age. Seraphina lies buried in the former cathedral, St. Stephen's Church, where she began her religious life. The cause of her beatification was introduced in Rome in 1769, but was suspended in the troubles of the Church at the end of the century. An attempt to revive the cause in 1865 was unsuccessful.

Seraphina's foundations were conservatories which educated girls, but for all intents and purposes were cloistered monasteries. Her sisters wore the Carmelite habit, recited the canonical office according to the Roman rite, kept the cloister, and observed the perfect common life. In 1676 and 1692 Seraphina requested papal cloister, but in each case met with refusal. Only after her death did this development take place. In 1747 Capri received papal cloister; by that time at least Nocera (1716) and Anacapri had achieved that condition. In the cloistered monasteries the sisters made vows instead of an oblation. There was no central administration, though a certain precedence and authority was accorded the Capri community and its prioress.

For her foundations Seraphina adopted the Carmelite rule of 1247. She received the inspiration for them in the Carmine Maggiore of Naples, and her spirit was closely modelled on St. Teresa. Yet she worked quite independently of the two Carmelite Orders. She looked for help elsewhere, especially the Oratory, and insisted on placing her houses under the bishops, to whom the sisters made their oblation. With time, however, the Congregation drew closer to the old Carmel, perhaps through the postulator of the Order, Seraphim Potenza (1697-1763), a member of the Carmine of Naples with the same given name as the foundress, who initiated the cause of her beatification and seems to have had a part in drawing up constitutions for the Congregation.

The vitality of Seraphina's institutions lingered after her death. Fisciano first gave rise to a foundation in Castel San Giorgio (1710). From Capri itself were founded Santa Maria Capua Vetere (1710), Marigliano (1715), Tramonti (1723), Bagnoli (1725), Sarno (1732). Torre del Greco issued in Novi Velia (1721); Massalubrense, in Sant'Angelo a Fasanella (1729) and St. Teresa's in Naples (1734). Other houses are known to have existed in Camigliano, Ripacandida and Frasso (1741), and the list may not be complete.

According to the bishop of Calvi, the Theatine Joseph Capece Zurlo, later Cardinal of Naples, the sisters of Camigliano were "little instructed in the duties of their rule and the devotion they owed to the most Holy Virgin under this title of Carmel." From Naples accordingly he fetched a preacher of missions who among other measures commissioned a bas-relief of Our Lady of Mount Carmel (1777) which became the object of universal devotion.

The brief existence of the conservatory of Marigliano terminated in 1723 over differences with Duchess Isabella Mastrillo, with her husband Duke John, lords of the place, but the foundation was none the less significant due to the fact that there in 1718, Mary Celeste Crostarosa received the Carmelite habit and the name Colomba of the Holy Spirit. After the dissolution of the conservatory Mary Celeste went on to found her own Order of Redemptorist Nuns which bears more than one trace of the Carmelite sojourn of its foundress. St. Alphonsus himself knew and esteemed Sr. Seraphina's rule and provided spiritual ministry to several of her foundations.

With few exceptions the conservatories of the Congregation of the Most Holy Savior fell victims to the Napoleonic suppression in Italy. Only Fisciano, Massalubrense, and Nocera dei Pagani—the first a Carmelite, the other two Discalced Carmelite monasteries—are all that remain of Seraphina's tireless efforts.

Sr. Seraphina's daughters led lives of intense prayer and many of them experienced mystical states. They all practiced the most ferocious penances which often shattered their health and today provoke knowing smiles in the psychological profession as well as some of the less felicitous paragraphs in Norman Douglas' *Siren Land*. It is difficult to identify the human persons in the pious fog raised by 17th century biographers. Somewhat more skillful than most was Letizia of Heaven (1661-1737), prolific chronicler of her sisters' lives. More flowery is the style of another biographer, Gaudiosa of the Holy Spirit (*fl.* 1743).

Of the original community of Capri, Teresa Martorelli (1651-1722) was the daughter of Candida Pisa, a cousin of Sr. Seraphina. With her brother and sister she was adopted by Don Ottavio Pisa after the pestilence in Naples of 1656 had removed her parents. All three children became religious. Mark Martorelli became a Jesuit; Teresa and her sister Olympia joined Sr. Prudence in founding the monastery of the Most Holy Savior on Capri. In 1672, Teresa was given the name Ammirabile of the Solitude. Fr. Vincent Avinatri held her in high regard and ordered her to commit her spiritual experiences to writing. In 1689, Seraphina sent her to Nocera, where she was immediately elected prioress, an office she filled for nine years. During that time she erected a wall around the garden, thus enabling the monastery to accept papal enclosure. She used to help the workers building the wall and became as dark as a Moor. During her last illness she was assisted by her confessor Francis Castelli and visited by Bishop Dominic Galisio, of Lettere, benefactor of the community and spiritual son of Sr. Seraphina.

Christina Bucci (1646-1722) was born in Naples, the daughter of Anthony and Victoria Bucci. Her older sister Mathilda was associated with the foundress of the Dominican monastery of Bethlehem in the same city. The pestilence of 1656 left of the family only Christina and her mother who gave her into the care of a Dominican tertiary, Sr. Cecily Tedesco. When five years later Prudence Pisa enlisted Sr. Cecily for her new foundation on Capri, it was agreed that Christina might accompany her governess. The other member of the community, Anna Alfano, was of Christina's age, and the two girls vied with each other in generous dedication to religious life. It was Christina, become Diletta of Jesus, whom Seraphina chose to accompany her in founding Vico in 1676 and to become its first prioress at the age of thirty. There Diletta spent the rest of her long life, by instruction and example placing the foundation on a solid footing.

Associated with Diletta in the founding of Vico was Gaetana Brancaccio (1653-1699), born in Naples of well-to-do parents. Her father Caspar, belonged to a confraternity of merchants attached to the church of the Oratorians and so came to know of Sr. Seraphina and her work on Capri. In 1665 he entrusted his daughters Dorothy and Gaetana to her care. Dorothy died as an *educanda,* Sr. Seraphina herself writing an account of her precocious sanctity. Gaetana in 1668 received the habit and the name Avventurata of Mary, for her devotion to the Virgin. Her practical sense indicated her for the office of *dispensiera* (1672). In Vico she took over the task of novice mistress. Her gifts were also of value in the construc-

143

tion of the monastery. The workers with whom she modestly and prudently treated looked on this young nun as another St. Agnes of Montepulciano. At thirty-two Avventurata became prioress. "With regard to the rest of her life," writes her biographer, Sr. Letizia of Heaven, "consult the Oratorians, and specifically Fr. (Thomas) Pagano, have them fetch you the Book of Foundations of Mother Seraphina and you will find the rest (of her life) and happy death."

Anna Alfano (1643-1683) was the native of Capri in the original community, daughter of John Baptist Alfano and Constance Strina, humble tillers of the soil. The pestilence of 1656 vaulted the strip of sea between Naples and Capri to convert the island paradise into an inferno. Left an orphan with her two younger brothers, Anna was adopted by her uncles. A providential meeting occurred when Anna, afflicted with ringworm, was sent for treatment to Sr. Prudence who included this service among her many charitable activities on behalf of the poor. This contact was probably not the last; in any case when Prudence opened her conservatory, Anna, who had been leading a celibate life, immediately joined her. With the four others she made her solemn oblation, October 11, 1662. Later she received the name Illuminata of the Truth. In the new foundation she proved most useful in spite of her lack of education. She worked in the kitchen, acted as portress and at various times was placed in charge of laysisters, *educande* and novices. She was in effect the right hand of the foundress who made her vicaress in her absence.

To recruit candidates for her undertaking Seraphina levied heavily on her family, numerous in spite of the ravages of pestilence. Bonaventura of St. Philip (1617-1690) was related to Seraphina through her maternal grandmother. Like her she was born in Naples of a wealthy merchant family who did not object to her living alone as a *pinzocchera* in the habit of the Jesuits. Her spiritual directors were Oratorians. After the pestilence of 1656, in which her parents perished, she joined her sister Victoria Scoppa in a house attached to the Church of St. Lawrence from which they could attend functions through a window. In 1661, Seraphina persuaded her to enter her monastery on Capri. There

VENER. M. SOR. SERAPHINA DE DEO
Quæ Diuina charitate flagrans
euolavit ad Sponsum die 17 Martij 1699
Ætatis suæ An. 78

Seraphina af God, 1621-1649,
foundress of the Congregation of the Most Holy Savior.
Engraving by Andrew Mailar, 1722.

A gathering of Carmelites,
Careggi - Italy

she continued her life of assiduous prayer. The last two years of her life were passed in severe spiritual aridity. In her last agony she was deprived of the comfort of the presence of Seraphina who was confined to her cell by the Holy Office.

Giacoma Pisa (1624-1692), the daughter of Carlo Antonio Pisa, was Seraphina's cousin. At sixteen she retired from the world, placed herself under the direction of the Jesuits and took their habit. Whenever she visited Naples from Capri, Seraphina stayed with this family, finding its devout atmosphere congenial. The condition of her ailing mother made it impossible for Giacoma to join her cousin in her monastery on Capri. Subsequently Giacoma married twice and on the death of her second husband entered the monastery of the Most Holy Savior with two nieces (1676). At her clothing she received the name Felice Fortuna. One of her nieces, Crocifissa of the Love of God, preceded her in death at the age of twenty.

Fortunata of Heaven (1659-1717) was Seraphina's niece, the daughter of her sister Ursula who married Christopher Smimer, a German resident in Naples. From her infancy Fortunata was destined for religious life. Her aunt persuaded her parents to lodge her on Capri with her cousin Julius Pisa, canon of the Cathedral, and his sister Laudonia Pisa, a Jesuit tertiary. As soon as possible, at the age of nine, she was brought into the monastery and at the canonical age of fifteen was clothed in the habit. Fortunata became an excellent religious, prioress of Capri and foundress in 1714 of Santa Maria Capua Vetere.

Sister Laudonia was also implicated in the vocation of Rose del Giardino Gesù (1650-1721), native of Capri. At first Rosa was not able to enter the conservatory of the Most Holy Savior, because as the eldest she was needed in her widowed father's house. On Laudonia's recommendation she was admitted at the age of sixteen and clothed in the habit as a laysister (1668). It was she whom Seraphina chose to be her guardian during her confinement to her cell by the Holy Office.

Also of the Capri conservatory, Ursula d'Avenia (1655-1704) was the eldest of five children, two boys and three girls. When the widowed mother remarried, the children were placed in the care of her brother-in-law,

Charles d'Avenia, a priest. He decided that Ursula should marry and the two younger girls become religious, through he had his doubts about the youngest, for she was disfigured by smallpox. The one chosen to become a nun, Violante, at first refused to hear the matter spoken of, but eventually entered the monastery on Capri as Gaudiosa of the Spirit. Ursula undertook the charge of her uncle's household and her two younger brothers and gave no thought to religious life. However she too changed her mind and in 1676, a late vocation at twenty-one, over the protests of her uncle and the pleas of her brothers, entered the same monastery as Splendida of the Savior.

The conservatory of the Most Holy Savior had been established hardly more than a year, when Sr. Seraphina one morning answered a knock at the door to find there Anastasia, a child of seven, who declared that she wanted to become a num. When the parents, Thomas and Grace Cardona, later arrived to fetch her home, Anastasia set up such a wail that it was finally agreed that she could remain as an *educanda*. Clothed in the habit at the age of fifteen (1670), she was two years later given the name of Emerald of the Splendor, one of Seraphina's more fanciful flights in nomenclature, which mercifully was later changed to Anna Teresa of the Bl. Trinity. In 1685, at the age of thirty, she accompanied Sr. Seraphina and Gemma of Heaven to reform the conservatory at Torre del Greco and remained behind as prioress of the amalgamated community, a difficult task she laudably performed for thirty-six years. In the last year of a long life she founded Novi Velia (1721). She left an account of her journey from Capri to Torre and a number of poems.

Rosalia Ascione was already an inmate of the conservatory at Torre when Seraphina arrived to reform it. Her father, Francis Ascione, was born in Torre, but for his affairs lived in Rome, where he married Elizabeth del Canto, native of that city. A devout man, he visited the shrine of St. Rosalia during a trip to Palermo and was so impressed by her legend that he bestowed her name on the daughter his wife presented him with in 1656. As a young girl Rosalia was taken up with the interests and amusements of her age, but after the family moved to Naples her father placed her, aged twenty-three, in the Dominican conservatory in his native Torre. She was won over by the Carmelite reformer and in 1685 was the first to receive the habit of the Order in the reconstituted community. She also received the name Fiorita, happily changed to Seraphina of Jesus. Several times she was placed in charge of the novices and *educande*. For many years she patiently suffered chronic illness until her death in 1719.

Fisciano remembers Bonaventura of St. Joseph for holiness of life. Her father, Julius Pacifico, was a prosperous business man of Naples, which is a wonder, for he spent more time in church than in the counting-house. His twelve children too were inclined to piety and religion. Of the eight girls, three became cloistered Dominican nuns in Lettere, another donned the Dominican tertiary habit. The fifth daughter, Anna, born in 1673, as the eldest was destined for the married state, but when her two younger sisters, Petronilla and Rosa, were indicated for religious life, Anna begged to be allowed to join them. The convent recommended by their maternal uncle, the Capuchin Cajetan of Naples, was the newly founded conservatory of St. Joseph in Fisciano. The foundresses were Archangela Fortunata, prioress; Gaudiosa of the Holy Spirit, vicaress; and Letizia of Heaven, mistress of novices. On October 14, 1692, Anna received the Carmelite habit and the name Bonaventura of St. Joseph. When the monastery received a picture of Sr. Seraphina on her death, Bonaventura prayed God to be given her spirit. She received a cross to bear in the form of severe chronic headaches, an affliction she cheerfully bore until her early death in 1705.

Appendix 2

SOME GENERAL REFERENCES

Boaga, Emanuele, O. Carm. *In obsequio Iesu Christi; commento alle costituzioni delle monache carmelitane*. Roma, 1981.

Brenninger, Joannes a Cruce, O.Carm. *Il Monte Carmelo*. (A circular letter to Carmelite nuns.) Roma, 1945.

"Carmelicola." "Moniales nostrae," *Vinculum*, 3 (1952-1953), 174-6.

Catena, Claudio, O.Carm. "Le donne nel Carmelo italiano," *Carmelus*, 10 (1963), 9-55.

————. *Le Carmelitane; storia e spiritualità*. Roma, 1969.

Catta, E. "Observance et spiritualité chez les Carmélites non thérésiennes en Bretagne à la vielle de la Révolution," *Actes du 76e Congrès des Sociétés Savantes*. Rennes, 1951, 48-71.

Daniel a Virgine Maria, O.Carm. *Vinea Carmeli*. Antwerpen, 1662, 544-60.

Limcaco, Fidelis, O.Carm. "Brevis conspectus historicus monasteriorum monialium II Ordinis nunc existentium," *Analecta Ordinis Carmelitarum*, 19 (1954), 24-28, 46-52, 71-74, 88-91, 103-6. In collaboration with Albertus Groeneveld, O.Carm.

————. "Moniales nostrae," *Vinculum*, 3 (1952-1953), 271-6.

López Melús, Rafael M., O. Carm. *Como ellas*. Barcelona, Juan Flors, 1957.

Martino, Alberto, O.Carm. "Monasteri femminili del Carmelo attraverso i secoli," *Carmelus*, 10 (1963), 263-312.

Saggi, Ludovico, O.Carm. "Originale bulla 'Cum nulla' qua Nicolaus Papa V canonice instituit II et III Ordines Carmelitarum," *Analecta Ordinis Carmelitarum*, 17 (1952), 3-5.

Staring, Adrianus, O.Carm. "The Carmelite Sisters in the Netherlands," *Carmelus*, 10 (1963), 56-92.

Steggink, Otger, O.Carm. "Beaterios y monasterios Carmelitas españoles en los siglos XV y XVI," *Carmelus*, 10 (1963), 149-231.

──────. *La reforma del Carmelo español; la vísita canónica del general Rubeo y su encuentro con Santa Teresa (1566-1567)*. Roma, 1965.

Wilderink, Vitalis, O.Carm. "Les premiers monastères de Carmélites en France," *Carmelus*, 10 (1963), 93-148.

──────. *Les constitutions des premières Carmélites en France*. Rome, 1966.

Velasco, Balbino, O.Carm. "¿Monjas carmelitas en Barcelona en 1346?" *Carmelus*, 32 (1985), 190-2.

Villiers, Cosmas de, O.Carm. *Bibliotheca carmelitana* (2 v., Aurelianis, 1725). Offset ed. by Gabriel Wessels, O.Carm. Roma, 1927; II, 1009: Virgineus Carmeli sanctimonialium scriptis illustrium chorus.

Appendix 3

PUBLISHED MATERIALS
ON INDIVIDUAL MONASTERIES

Allentown, Pa.

Dolan, Albert H., O.Carm. *In the Valley of St. Therese; a Description of the Life and Work of the Carmelite Sisters of Allentown.* Chicago, 1938.

Dressel, Anthony C., O.Carm. "History of the Carmelite Monastery of St. Therese, Little Flower of Jesus, and St. Mary Magdalen di Pazzi, Ancient Observance, Lanark Manor, Allentown, Pa.," *The Sword*, 3 (1939), 496-9; 4 (1940), 40-52.

The First Twenty-Five Silver Years of the Carmel of Allentown. Allentown, Pa., 1956.

Mother Therese and the Carmel of Allentown, by a member of the community. Philadelphia, Pa., 1949.

Anacapri

Campana, E. "Il 'paradiso terrestre' ad Anacapri," *Il Monte Carmelo*, 16 (1930), 273-6.

Chiminelli Piero. "Il 'paradiso terrestre' in San Michele di Anacapri," *Il Monte Carmelo*, 30 (1944), 36-39.

Aracena.

"Benedición del monasterio restaurado de Madres Carmelitas de Aracena," *El Santo Escapulario*, 59 (1963), 519-20.

Avila

González y González, Nicolás. *El monasterio de la Encarnación de Avila.* Avila, 1976-1977. 2 v.

Pinel y Monroy, María, O.Carm. *Retablo de Carmelitas*; ed. Nicolás González. Madrid, 1981.

Zimmerman, Benedict, O.C.D. "El convento de la Encarnación de Avila," *El Monte Carmelo*, (1910), 259-65.

Barcelona

Angel de la Guardia (*pseud.*). "Las Carmelitas de la semana roja," *El Santo Escapulario*, 16 (1919), 335-43, etc.

"Breve relación de la milagrosa imágen de la Santísima Virgen que se venera en el ermita del huerto del convento de religiosas Carmelitas calzadas de Barcelona," *Revista carmelitana,* 8 (1884), 94-95.

Paulí Meléndez, Antonio. "El monasterio de la Encarnación," *El Santo Escapulario,* 33 (1936), 44-49.

————. *El monasterio de la Encarnación, M.M. Carmelitas de Barcelona.* Barcelona, 1951.

Soler y Garigosa, Lino, "Bendición solemne de la nueva iglesia del convento de las Carmelitas Calzadas de Las Corts, cerca de Barcelona," *Revista carmelitana,* 10 (1886), 4-7.

Boxmeer, « Elzendaal »

Wuisman, G. "Het Carmelitessenklooster Elzendaal te Boxmeer, Sept. 1672 - Sept. 1922," *Bossche Bijdragen,* 5 (1923), 1-44.

Brugge

Waele, W. H. J. "Le couvent des Soeurs de Notre-Dame, dit de Sion à Bruges," *Le Beffroi,* 3 (1866-1870), 46-53, etc.

Camerino

Loreti, Ferruccio. *Il Carmelo di Camerino; pagine di storia e di cronaca.* Camerino, 1977.

Camigliano

Breve relazione dell'immagine miracolosa... che si venera... in Camigliano... Napoli, 1787.

Cañete la Real

Un Carmelita. "El convento de monjas Carmelitas de la A. O. de Cañete la Real," *El Santo Escapulario,* 43 (1947), 28-29, etc.

Rodríguez, Fernando María, O.Carm. "Tercer centenario de la fundación del monasterio de Carmelitas de la A. O. de Cañete la Real (Málaga)," *El Santo Escapulario,* 59 (1963), 132-3, 170-1.

Capua

Chillemi, Rosolino. *Una falsa congiuntura borbonica a Capua.* Capua, 1970. Extract from *Capys.*

Ciney

Barbier, V. *Les Carmélites de Ciney*. Louvain, 1884.

Firenze. Santa Maria degli Angeli.

Breve ragguaglio della produzione prodigiosa d'olio seguita o scoperta il dì 30 maggio 1806... ad intercessione della B. Maria Bartolommea Bagnesi... Firenze, 1807.

Caioli, Paolo, O.Carm. "I primi monasteri di Carmelitane e le prime compagnie di terziari carmelitani in Firenze," *Analecta Ordinis Carmelitarum*, 18 (1953), 3-55.

Catena, Claudio, O.Carm. *Santa Maria Maddalena de' Pazzi, carmelitana; orientamenti spirituali e ambiente in cui visse.* Roma, 1966.

"Cinque secoli di vita carmelitana a Santa Maria degli Angeli," *Il Monte Carmelo*, 36 (1950), 136-47.

"Una gloria carmelitana, il monastero di S. M. degli Angeli," *Il Monte Carmelo*, 11 (1925), 99-101, etc.

M. P. di Gesù. "L'origine del monastero di S. Maria degli Angeli," *Il Monte Carmelo*, 23 (1937), 46-50.

Fisciano

"Il Carmelo di Fisciano," *I Trionfi della Bruna*, 2 (1953), 109-12.

Carroll, Eamon, O.Carm. "Visit to Fisciano," *The Sword*, 15 (1952), 467-73.

Monaco, Gabriele, O.Carm. "Il Carmelo di Fisciano sotto la tormenta," *Il Monte Carmelo*, 33 (1947), 77-78.

Huy

Cohen, Gustave. *Nativités et moralités liégeoises du moyen-age.* Bruxelles, 1953.

Jesi

Boaga, Emanuele, O.Carm. *"Le Grazie" e il Carmelo di Jesi.* Roma, 1981.

————. *Le Carmelitane di Jesi; appunti di storia e spiritualità.* Jesi, 1985.

Martino, Alberto, O.Carm. "Il monastero delle Carmelitane di Iesi annesso al monumentale tempio di S. Marco," *La Madonna del Carmine*, 14 (1960), 212-4.

Stella, Pietro, O.Carm. "Le Carmelitane in Iesi," *Il Monte Carmelo*, 26 (1940), 199-201.

Madrid. La Baronesa

Velasco, Balbino, O.Carm. *El convento de Carmelitas de la Baronesa de Madrid*. Madrid, 1980. Offprint from *Anales del Instituto de Estudios Madrileños*, v. 17.

Madrid. Las Maravillas

Montalbán, José Joaquín. "Discurso histórico-sagrado de N. S. de las Maravillas," *Revista carmelitana*, 11 (1887), 175-7, 188-95.

Pérez de Guzmán, Juan. "En el convento de Las Maravillas; recuerdos del dos de mayo de 1808," *Revista carmelitana*, 14 (1890), 71-74.

Suárez y Munano, Pedro de Alcántara. *Historia de la sagrada imagen de Ntra. Sra. la Real de las Maravillas, que se venera en su real convento de religiosas Carmelitas Recoletas de Madrid*. Lérida, 1874.

Velasco, Balbino, O.Carm. "El convento de las Carmelitas de Nuestra Señora de las Maravillas de Madrid," *Carmelus*, 23 (1976), 119-53.

Marigliano

Tellería, Ramón, C.SS.R. "Ven. Sororis Mariae Coelestis Crostarosa experientia prima religiosa apud conservatorium SS. Joseph et Teresiae in oppido Mariliani (Marigliano), 1718-1723," *Spicilegium Historicum C.SS.R.*, 12 (1964), 79-128.

Messina

Quagliarella, Pier Tommaso. *Un atto notarile dell'epoca sveva (1263) riguardante le suore carmelitane di Messina*. Messina, 1965. Extract from *Archivio Storico Messinese*, 3a ser., v. 15-16 (1964-1965).

Napoli. Santa Croce

D'Ambra, Raffaele. *Santa Croce di Lucca delle suore carmelitane*. Napoli, 1888.

" Il Carmelo della S. Croce di Lucca di Napoli," *Trionfi della Bruna*, 22 (1953), 122-6.

Santolla, Angelo, O.Carm. " 'La croce di Lucca'—le monache carmelitane in Napoli," *Il Monte Carmelo*, 8 (1922), 251-3.

Napoli. Santissimo Sacramento.

Fornari, Gioacchino. *Brevi cenni storici intorno alla chiesa di "S. Maria Maddalena dei Pazzi del SSmo. Sacramento" in Napoli.* Napoli, 1934.

Mastelloni, Andrea, O.Carm. *La prima chiesa dedicata a S. Maria Maddalena de Pazzi, carmelitana.* Napoli, 1675.

Parma

Saggi, Ludovico, O.Carm. "Prima notitia de monialibus Ordinis in civitate Parma," *Analecta Ordinis Carmelitarum,* 20 (1956-1957), 197-8.

Piedrahita

Velasco, Balbino, O.Carm. "Un lienzo de Alonso Cano en Piedrahita (Avila)," *Boletín del Seminario de Estudios de Arte y Arquelogía,* 46 (1980), 500-4.

Ravenna

Cenni storici sulle carmelitane di Ravenna in occasione del primo centenario di clausura papale. Ravenna, 1940.

"Il monastero delle carmelitane di Ravenna," *Il Monte Carmelo,* 26 (1940), 249-54.

Sabatini, Andrea, O.Carm. *Le carmelitane a Ravenna; memorie storiche del monastero edite in occasione del bicentenario della sua fondazione, 1773-1973.* Ravenna, 1973.

Rennes

Pocquet de Haut-Jussé, B.-A. *L'ancien monastère des Carmélites de Rennes.* Rennes, 1956. Extract from *Bulletin et Mémoires de la Société Archéologique d'Ille-et-Villaine,* v. 70.

San Juan, P. R.

Dávila, Arturo. "José Campeche y sus hermanos en el convento de las carmelitas," *Revista del Istituto de Cultura Puertorriqueña,* 2 (1959), no. 2, p. 12-17.

Tárrega

Basagañas, Bautista M., O.Carm. "Benedición e inauguración de la nueva iglesia de las monjas carmelitas de Tárrega (Lérida)," *El Santo Escapulario,* 53 (1957), 22-24, 356-7.

Utrera

"Bodas de diamante del monasterio de la Purísima Concepción de Utrera (Sevilla), 1888-1963," *El Santo Escapulario,* 59 (1963), 215-6.

Valencia. Encarnación

"Acontecimiento milagroso en el convento de la Encarnación de religiosas Carmelitas Calzadas de Valencia," *Revista carmelitana,* 9 (1885), 181-3, 195, 221.

Vannes

Le Mené, Joseph Marie. *Les Carmélites de Vannes.* Vannes, 1897.

Smet, Joachim, O.Carm. "The Psalter of Blessed Frances of Amboise," *The Sword,* 11 (1947), 96-99.

Vetralla

Boaga, Emanuele, O.Carm. *San Paolo della Croce, predicazione di esercizi spirituali alle religiose.* Roma, 1982.

"El Cardenal Tardini y las Carmelitas de Vetralla," *El Santo Escapulario,* 58 (1962), 14-15.

"Il 'Carmelo' di Vetralla distrutto da bombe aeree," *Il Monte Carmelo,* 30 (1944), 54-56.

Merangoni, Giovanni. *Compendio della vita di D. Benedetto Baldi da Vetralla.* Roma, 1712.

Paolucci, Francesco. *Vita del Servo di Dio Benedetto Baldi di Vetralla, fondatore nella sua patria del monastero delle Carmelitane di S. Maria Maddalena de' Pazzi.* Roma, 1892.

Possanzini, Stefano, O.Carm. *L'ambiente del monastero "Monte Carmelo" di Vetralla al tempo di San Paolo della Croce.* Roma, 1980.

———. *Il monastero Monte Carmelo di Vetralla, storia e spiritualità.* Vetralla, 1982.

Relazione della miracolosa moltiplicazione di farina operata da Dio per intercessione di San Luigi Gonzaga... 1729... Viterbo, 1875.

Revelli, Mariz. "Il 'Carmelo' di Vetralla e S. Paolo della Croce," *Il Monte Carmelo,* 27 (1941), 104-7.

———. "San Luigi Gonzaga e il Carmelo di Vetralla," *Il Monte Carmelo,* 26 (1940), 133-5.

Vilvoorde

Caruana, Elia, O.Carm. "La prodigiosa immagine di Maria Consolatrice nel monastero delle Carmelitane di Vilvorde," *Il Monte Carmelo*, 16 (1930), 173-7, 202-5.

Christiaens, Jozef. "Enkele muziekhandschriften in karmelitaans bezit," *Ons Geestelijk Erf*, 50 (1976), 425-33.

Compaignon, I. *Histoire admirable de Notre Dame de Consolation révérée dans l'église du monastère des religieuses Carmélites de Vilvoorde.* Bruxelles, 1648.

Marijnissen, R. "Onze Lieve Vrouw ten Troost van Vilvoorde, onderzoek en behandeling," *Bulletin de l'Institut Royal du Patrimoine Artistique*, 4 (1961), 77-95.

Vanderspeeten, H. P., S. J. *Notre Dame de Consolation, notice historique sur la statue miraculeuse de la Sainte Vierge vénérée sous ce nom dans l'église des Carmélites Chaussées à Vilvoorde.* Bruxelles, 1878.

Wessels, Gabriel, O.Carm. "Imago Divae Consolatricis apud moniales carmelitas in Vilvoorde (Belgio)," *Analecta Ordinis Carmelitarum*, 5 (1923-1926), 70-75.

Wahpeton

Carmel of Mary, Description of the Life and Work of the Cloistered Carmelite Nuns of the Ancient Observance in the Diocese of Fargo. Allentown, Pa., 1955.

Zenderen

Lokkers, Adalbertus, O.Carm. "De convento Zenderensi S. Joseph monialium Ordinis nostri," *Analecta Ordinis Carmelitarum*, 10 (1938-1940), 304-5.

Appendix 4

PUBLISHED MONOGRAPHS AND ARTICLES ON NUNS

A rich source of biographical information on Carmelite nuns is the Archive of the Postulator General of the Order, especially the manuscript collection made by the postulator, Serafino Potenza, in the second quarter of the 18th century. Obviously, this source is available only to a limited number of readers. Below are listed (non-beatified or canonized) nuns whose lives have been the subject of separate monographs and articles.

Amarillo, María Josefa de la Encarnación, 1811-1891.

T. del S.S.M. "Apuntes biográficos de la virtuosa Madre María Josefa de la Encarnación Amarillo, Carmelita Calzada del convento de Osuna," *Revista carmelitana*, 16 (1892), 245-7, 249.

Badía Flaquer, María del Patrocinio de San José, 1903-1936.

Sánchez Carracedo, Hilarión M., O.Carm. *La azucena de Vich; vida de Sor María del Patrocinio de San José Badía Flaquer, religiosa carmelita del monasterio de la Presentación de Vich, martirizada por las hordas rojas*, 2a ed. Vich, 1947.

Balart Murgadas, Isabel del Santísimo Sacramento, d. 1724.

Cabrer, José, O.Carm. "La V.M. Isabel del Santísimo Sacramento," *Revista carmelitana*, 10 (1886), 135-7.

Berti, Maria Maddalena.

"La beniamina di S. Maria Maddalena de' Pazzi (Maria de' Berti)," *Il Monte Carmelo*, 32 (1946), 50-51.

Boattini, Teresa Eletta Maddalena dello Spirito Santo, 1851-1885.

Memorie di Elvira Boattini, in religione Suor Teresa Eletta Maddalena dello Spirito, del monastero di S. Maria Maddalena de' Pazzi in Firenze. Prato, 1887.

157

Bonastre, Serafina Andrea, *d.* **1649.**

Lumbier, Raimundo. *Vida de la venerable Madre Sor Serafina Andrea Bonastre, fundadora principal del Convento de la Encarnación de Zaragoça.* Zaragoça, 1673.

Carrasco, Cristobalina de Jesús Crucificado, 1646-1739.

Mata, Francesca de, O.Carm. "Una gloria de Antequera, la V.M. Cristobalina de Jesús Crucificado Carrasco, Carmelita Calzada," *Revista carmelitana,* 14 (1890), 10-11, etc.

Contugi, Dianora, 1531-1579.
Contugi, Vittoria, 1532-1595.

Teresa del Bambino Gesù, O.Carm. "Due privilegiate di Maria," *Il Monte Carmelo,* 36 (1950), 149-50.

Corsini, Maria Maddalena Gertrude, *d.* **1807.**

Elogio, o sia, breve ragguaglio della vita e morte preziosa della Molto Reverenda Madre Suor Maria Maddalena Corsini... Firenze, 1808.

Del Giocondo, Francesca, 1572-1642.

"Ginevra del Giocondo (novizia di S. Maria Maria Maddalena de' Pazzi)," *Il Monte Carmelo,* 28 (1942), 168-70.

Escobar y Villalba, Margarita, 1608-1641.
Escobar y Villalba, Maria, 1599-1634.
Escobar y Villalba, Mariana, 1603-1660.

Faci, Roque Alberto, O.Carm. *Vida de la V. Mariana Villalba y Vicente y las de sus tres hijas, Sor Maria, Sor Margarita, y Sor Mariana Escobar.* Pamplona, 1761.

López Melús, Rafael, O.Carm. *Bajo el manto de la madre; doctrina mariana de Sor Maria Escobar y Villalba, Carmelita contemplativa de la Encarnación de Zaragoza (1599-1634).* Caudete, 1978.

Eulalia de la Cruz Mora y Xammar, 1669-1725.

Martí Albanell, Federico. *Compendio de la vida de la Sierva de Dios, Madre Eulalia de la Cruz, religiosa del convento de Carmelitas de la Encarnación de Barcelona (1669-1725).* Barcelona, 1931.

Falangola, Maria Teresa, 1835-1908.

Pagliara, Flaviano. *Per la morte di Maria Teresa Falangola, priora delle Suore Carmelitane, avenuta il 27 novembre 1908, elogio funebre.* Castellamare, 1908.

Gesualda Eletta dello Spirito Santo, 1879-1930.

Suor Gesualda dello Spirito Santo. Roma, 19--.

Gianfigliazzi, Caterina.

"Caterina Gianfigliazzi, novizia di S. Maria Maddalena de' Pazzi," *Il Monte Carmelo*, 29 (1943), 23-24.

Giovannini, Francesca Teresa dei Santi Angeli, 1837-1903.

Gallerani, Alessandro S. J. *La Madre Francesca Teresa dei Santi Angeli, al secolo Elena Giovannini, del v. monastero di S. M. Maddalena de' Pazzi in Firenze...* Modena, 1903.

Koning, Josephine, 1863-1931.

Driessen, Eugenius, O.Carm. "Madre Giuseppina Koning, carmelitana," *Il Monte Carmelo*, 27 (1941), 137-40.

Smet, Joachim, O.Carm. "Mother Josephine Koning, O.Carm., the Little Flower of Holland (1863-1931)," *The Sword*, 3 (1939), 439-43; 4 (1940), 25-27.

———. *A Passion Flower of Carmel.* Chicago, 1940.

Stegge, Pius aan de, O.Carm. *Een vrouw wijst de weg; het leven van Moeder Josephine, Carmelites, 1863-1931.* Heerlen, 1947.

Liguori, Teresa Maria, 1704-1724.

Alphonsus de Liguori, *Saint.* "Notes on the Life and Death of the Servant of God, Sister Teresa Mary de Liguori, Religious of the Monastery of the Blessed Sacrament in Naples"; *Complete Ascetical Works* (22 v., New York, 1886-1897), XI (1888), 299-318 (The Century Edition).

Maddalena Angelica, 1898-1920.

Volo di un'angelo, Suor Maddalena Angelica del monastero di S.M.M. de' Pazzi in Firenze. Torino, 1934.

Manzari, Rosaria di Santa Filomena, 1865-1935.

Semerano, Ferdinando. *Madre Rosaria di Santa Filomena del Carmelo di Ostuni.* Ostuni, 1935.

Maria Arcangela.

"Suor Maria Arcangiola, connovizia conversa di Santa M. Maddalena dei Pazzi," *Il Monte Carmelo,* 32 (1946), 6-13.

María de Jesús, 1589-1662.

Carrera Medina, José. *Vida de la venerable Madre María de Jesús y del Espino.* Madrid, 1872.

López Sendín, Alfonso, O.Carm. *Flor de Gredos; vida de la ven. M. María de Jesús y del Espino, Carmelita del Carmelo de la Madre de Dios de Piedrahita (Avila).* Avila, 1980.

Luis de Santa Teresa, O.Carm. *Vida de la Ven. Madre María de Jesús.* Salamanca, 1720.

Maria Grazia di Gesù, 1903-1931.

Teresa del Bambino Gesù, O.Carm. "Suor Maria Grazia di Gesù," *Roseti del Carmelo,* 6 (1953), 6-10, 20-21.

Maria Teresa del SS. Sacramento, 1870-1936.

Teresa del Bambino Gesù, O.Carm., "Maria Teresa del SS. Sacramento," *Roseti del Carmelo,* 6 (1953), 68-72.

Mariana da Purificação, 1623-1695.

Azevedo, Miguel de, O.Carm. *Memorial das instructivas palavras e edificantes obras de muito virtuosa Madre Marianna da Purificaçâo.* Lisboa, 1802.

Bruni, Mauricio, O.Carm. *Mariana da Purificaçâo (1623-1695), um fenomeno religioso de Portugal seiscentista.* Roma, 1956. 2 v. (Unpublished doctoral dissertation submitted to the Pontifical Gregorian University, Rome.)

Caetano de Vencimiento, O.Carm. *Fragmentos da prodigiosa vida da muito favorecida e amada esposa de Jesu Christo, a veneravel Madre Mariana da Purificaçam.* Lisboa, 1747.

Montalto, Maria Carmela della S. Trinità, 1688-1780.

Farrugia, Luigi. *Brevi cenni della vita di Suor Maria Carmela della SS. Trinità, nata Montalto-Gargallo, fondatrice del monastero delle Carmelitane di Siracusa.* Napoli, 1925.

Navarro, María Josefa de Jesús, *d.* **1625.**

Andrés, José, S.J. *Nueva maravilla de la gracia... Sor María Josepha de Jesús... religiosa de la Observancia de Nuestra Señora del Carmen en el convento de la Encarnación de Zaragoça.* Zaragoça, 1676.

Pascual y Jorba, Isabel de los Angeles, *d.* **1730.**

Cabrer, José, O.Carm. "La venerable M. Isabel de los Angeles," *Revista carmelitana,* 10 (1886), 150-2 (wrongly numbered 136-8).

Pazzi, Maria Cristina de', *d.* **1612.**

"Camilla de' Pazzi, novizia di S. Maria Maddalena de' Pazzi," *Il Monte Carmelo,* 29 (1943), 87-91, 106-9.

Perpetua da Luz, 1684-1736.

Brenninger, Joannes, O.Carm. "Maria Perpetua da Luz," *Analecta Ordinis Carmelitarum,* 12 (1943-1945), 6-115.

Martins, Mario, S.J. "Maria Perpetua de Luz," *Revue d'Ascétique et de Mystique,* 21 (1940), 149-76.

Pereira, José de Santa Ana, O.Carm. *Vida da insigne mestra de espirito, a virtuosa Madre Maria Perpetua da Luz.* Lisboa, 1742.

Picchi, Maria Maddalena di Gesù Sacramentato, 1841-1895.

Gallerani, Alessandro, S.J. *Memorie edificanti della Madre M. Maddalena Costante del SS. Sacramento, al secolo Adele Picchi... morta il 27 agosto 1895.* Modena, 1896-1897. 2 v. in 1.

Teresa del Bambino Gesù, O.Carm. "Madre Maria Maddalena Costante di Gesù Sacramentato," *Roseti del Carmelo,* 7 (1954), 87-90.

Pueyo y Pujadas, María de las Mercedes.

Triumphos del amor divino... Zaragoza, 1770. (*Vilancicos* on the occasion of her clothing.)

Salvatori, Maria Minima Luisa di Gesù Nazareno, 1780-1831.

Paolo di San Giuseppe, O.C.D. *Vita della Serva di Dio, la Madre Maria Minima Luisa di Gesù Nazareno... priora delle monache carmelitane nella città di Vetralla.* Roma, 1833.

Sanz Perea, María Magdalena de Pazzis, 1876-1953.

Datos para la vida de la Rvda. M. Magdalena de Pazzis Sanz Perea, Carmelita de la A. O. del convento de Utrea (Sevilla). 1956.

Serafina di Dio Pisa, 1621-1699.

D'Antonio, Giancrisostomo, O.F.M. *Madre Serafina di Dio.* Napoli, 1962.

Sguillante, Niccolò, C.Or. *Vita della venerabile Madre Suor Serafina di Dio, fondatrice di sette monasteri dell'Ordine carmelitano.* Proseguita e data alla luce dal P. Tommaso Pagani, C.Or. Venezia, 1743.

"La venerable Madre Serafina de Dios," *Revista carmelitana,* 2 (1877), 159-71, 179-81 ("traducido de italiano").

Wessels, Gabriel, O.Carm. "Vita ven. Seraphinae de Deo (ex processu beatificationis)," *Analecta Ordinis Carmelitarum,* 6 (1927-1929), 410-42.

Serafina di Sant'Antonio, 1868-1953.

Teresa del Bambino Gesù, O.Carm. "Luce nell'ombra, Sr. M. Serafina di S. Antonio," *Roseti del Carmelo,* 7 (1954), 6-8, 37-40.

Serio, Rosa Maria di Sant'Antonio, 1674-1726.

Boaga, Emanuele, O.Carm. "Le alterne vicende di un processo di beatificazione; il caso della Serva di Dio, Suor Rosa Maria Serio"; *Noscere sancta; miscellanea in memoria di Agostino Asnore, O.F.M. (m. 1982),* a cura di Isaac Vásquez Janeiro, O.F.M. (2 v., Roma, 1985), II, 385-428.

Gabriela vom H. Sacramento, O.C.D. *Leben der Ehrw. Rosa Maria Serio.* Innsbruck, 1903.

Gentili, Giuseppe, S.J. *Vita della venerabile Madre Rosa Maria Serio di S. Antonio.* Roma, 1738.

Quagliarella, Pier Tommaso, O.Carm. *Cenno biografico della Serva di Dio, Suor Rosa Maria Serio (Carmelitana), nata in Ostuni nel 1674 e morta in Fasano nel 1726.* Taranto, 1927.

Wessels, Gabriel, O.Carm. "Vita ven. Rosae Mariae Serio," *Analecta Ordinis Carmelitarum,* 2 (1911-1913), 20-26, etc.

Sommai, Francesca, 1580-1615.

"Francesca Sommai (novizia di S. M. Maddalena de' Pazzi," *Il Monte Carmelo,* 32 (1946), 81-86.

Strina, Illuminata della Verità, 1643-1683.

Farace, Salvatore. *Un eletto giglio caprese, ossia, Suor Illuminata della Verità...* Santa Maria Capua Vetere, 1935.

Strozzi, Minima di S. Filippo Neri, 1617-1672.

Luti, Mariano, O. Carm. "La vocazione di Camilla Strozzi (1617-1672)," *Il Monte Carmelo,* 36 (1950), 151-3.

Orlandini, Maria Serafica, O.Carm. *Breve ristretto della vita della venerabil Madre Suor Minima di S. Filippo Neri.* Lucca, 1717. Published anonymously.

Sylveira, Beatriz de, *d.* 1660.

Náxera, Manuel de, S.J. *Sermon en las sumptuosas exequias que celebrò el muy religioso convento de las Carmelitas Recoletas de Madrid, en 14 de febrero de 1660 a su fundadora la Señora Baronessa D. Beatrix de Sylveira.* Lisboa, 1661.

Therese of Jesus, 1877-1939.

Mother Therese and the Carmel of Allentown, by a member of the community. Philadelphia, 1949.

Torrente-Meléndez, María Lourdes del Santísimo Sacramento, 1916-1949.

Sánchez Carracedo, Hilarión, O.Carm. *Una víctima por los sacerdotes, Sor María Lourdes del Santísimo Sacramento, Carmelita de la Antiqua Observancia del monasterio de la Madre de Dio, de Piedrahita (1916-1948).* Zaragoza, 1950.

Trenta, Maria Maddalena.

"Re e suora: Federico IV di Danimarca e Suor M. Maddalena Trenta," *Il Monte Carmelo* 26 (1940), 159-62.

Verzin, Benedetta della Croce, *d.* **1976.**

Orrù, Giuseppe, O.Carm. *Cristo, mi confesso a te.* Roma, Gabriele Editore, 1979.

Vettori, Maria Benedetta, 1570-1598.

"Una novizia di S. Maria Maddalena de' Pazzi, Suor Maria Benedetta Vettori," *Il Monte Carmelo,* 28 (1942), 91-94, 105-9.

Ximénez, Caterina, *d.* **1617.**

"Caterina Ximénez, novizia di S. Maria Maddalena de' Pazzi," *Il Monte Carmelo,* 28 (1942), 119-23.